D1597648

THE ANGLER'S
BUCKET LIST

First published in the United States of America in 2023
by Universe Publishing, a division of
Rizzoli International Publications, Inc.
300 Park Avenue South
New York, NY 10010
www.rizzoliusa.com

2023 2024 2025 2026 / 10 9 8 7 6 5 4 3 2 1

ISBN: 978-0-7893-4147-1
Library of Congress Control Number: 2022949350

Visit us online:
Facebook.com/RizzoliNewYork
Twitter: @Rizzoli_Books
Instagram.com/RizzoliBooks
Pinterest.com/RizzoliBooks
YouTube.com/user/RizzoliNY
Issuu.com/Rizzoli

Conceived, designed, and produced by the Bright Press,
an imprint of the Quarto Group
1 Triptych Place
London SE1 9SH
United Kingdom
www.quarto.com

Publisher: James Evans
Editorial Director: Isheeta Mustafi
Managing Editor: Jacqui Sayers
Senior Editor: Joanna Bentley
Art Director: James Lawrence
Project Editor: Julie Brooke
Design: JC Lanaway
Picture Research: Sally Claxton, Jane Lanaway

Printed in China

THE ANGLER'S BUCKET LIST

500 GREAT FISHING ADVENTURES AROUND THE WORLD

RIVERS • LAKES • SHORES • DEEP SEA

JOHN BAILEY

with RAY BARTLETT, ROB BEATTIE,
KIKI DEERE, JOHNNY JENSEN

UNIVERSE

CONTENTS

INTRODUCTION

It was late summer 1995 and I was lying on the banks of the Shiskid River in northwest Mongolia. I was deep into my very first journey there and becoming as one with this vast land of winds, whispering forests, and echoing, empty spaces. The sky above me was achingly blue, the larch branches were alive with crossbills, and the huge, churning Shiskid at my feet promised a fishing adventure of a lifetime. It was early afternoon, quite warm but with the usual brisk breeze from the north, blowing off the mountains in Siberia and easing the remnants of a fading hangover.

Yesterday I had caught my first Mongolian taimen, a massive, almost mystical fish, and how we had celebrated, my herdsmen friends and I. We had drunk vodka under the star-studded sky. We had danced in the shadows thrown by the raging campfire. We had listened to a wolf cry from the snow-dusted hills and I had realized that life—an angler's life at least—really does not get much better than this. And I have never deviated from this belief.

Below | Peaceful fishing in Mongolia

Up for the challenge

The love of adventure is ingrained in every angler, the lure of exploration is essential to what we do. To the child fisher, the local pond and the neighboring stream offer untold thrills and challenges and the wanderlust only grows stronger as the years tick by. Perhaps a better word would be "waterlust": so many of us anglers want to discover rivers and lakes and seas at the very limits of the world and of our imagination. Perhaps we fisher-folk know better than anyone how magnificent this planet is. Take me. I have traveled to and fished in sixty-four countries worldwide and I can never remember being disappointed. In fact, the reverse is true. I just see visions of miracle waters on every continent where I have cast my line, and fish so spectacular they burn into your memory for life.

It is for this reason that I am so proud to be associated with this book, even though I stress I am only a part of an experienced team (see page 320). We have all traveled extensively and all succumbed to the call of the wild. But while adventure fishing is the most absorbing element of our sport, never underestimate its challenges. Danger never goes on vacation and only a fool fails to research every expedition properly and sets off ignorant of the issues that will be faced. We hope this book gives you a taste of the wonders to be enjoyed but always travel and fish with your eyes open and your senses alert.

It is important to add that angling venues are volatile and a good location can change quickly for all manner of reasons. For example, while writing this book, the war in Ukraine forced us to omit several tremendous salmon rivers that are now dangerous or politically out of bounds. Conservation initiatives can mean the suspension of fishing, and the changes in climate are also affecting many if not most regions of the world. Even fishing in the UK's River Wye was suspended in the summer of 2022 because of lack of rain, low flows, and oxygen depletion. So, whatever adventures you decide to explore, it is vital that you make yourself aware of the current situation in that country and on the river, lake, or ocean fishing ground you hope to visit.

The greatest catch

The fish themselves are at the heart of what adventure angling is all about and, my word, there are some wondrous creatures in this book! As you turn the pages, you'll see that we highlight some of the most iconic of these, fish that are amazing in every way. There's the ultimate deep sea trophy, black marlin; the king of freshwater fighters that still inhabits the jungle rivers of the subcontinent, the golden mahseer; the black bass, possibly the most intriguing fish that swims; the world's most glamorous catch, the Atlantic salmon, fished from the planet's most treasured rivers; the huge but rare Asian taimen; the Arctic char which, whether landlocked or sea running, features every color of the rainbow and presents a superb challenge; and the goliath tigerfish, a giant predator with teeth reminiscent of a saber-toothed tiger, which is perhaps the ultimate freshwater challenge.

The mouthwatering list goes on and on but we'd ask you to treat every fish as wondrous. There is a fish in Europe's rivers called the gudgeon. It weighs a millionth of a marlin but it is exquisitely colored along its flanks with sheens of blue, purple, and pewter and its fins are flecked a rich gold. Such love for all fish leads me to ask you to treat every capture with the care and respect even the smallest fish deserves. Remove fish from their habitat for as short a period as possible. Hold them with gentle, wetted hands. Weigh and photograph them with speed and release them with tender, loving care. If you do require a fish for the table, that is good too, but dispatch it quickly, cleanly, and never waste a mouthful.

Having said this, the angler who travels solely to catch fish will inevitably return no richer than when they left home. You can enjoy the fishing trip of a lifetime and catch nothing but memories. That is why these entries include, when they can, the importance of the method of fishing as well as the fish to be caught. Have you "dapped" for wild brown trout on an Irish lough? Or fished a popper for beasty black bass in the rain forests of Borneo and seen the river erupt before you? *How* you catch can be as important as *what* you catch. And there's more! The scenery can be so splendid that it feeds the soul and, of course, anglers soak it in at its best, at sunrise and sunset. Wildlife enhances every trip. Stay quiet and you'll find the birds will come to amaze and entertain you. Just as the children will in every village if you show an interest in their lives and a genuine wish to share in their world.

Right | **Using a guide will enable you to get the most from your trip**

Find an expert to guide you

Mentioning the humans who live alongside our fish brings us to the question of guides you might hire to help you. We hope the entries will give you a taste of what is out there and might even spark long-held angling dreams into action. However, in nearly all of these scenarios, your chances are increased if you are with an expert guide, local or not. Of course, if you are after goliath fish on the oceans, a captain and a crew will be central to your chances but the same is true for freshwaters. There are places where you can wander, sit down, and catch but these are in the minority. A good guide will show you the fish, teach you to catch them, alert you to the wildlife around you, and explain the history and culture of the region. They will become a friend—and will keep you safe. And never forget that, by employing one, you are stimulating the local economy and this can be an important element of conservation. When I first made it to the southern jungles of India, many if not most of the river people poisoned, netted, and dynamited the rivers for the fish they sold at market. It was a poor living that necessarily got poorer. But as the years progressed and the poachers became guides and friends, the fish were protected. The incomes of these families grew and sportfishing became ever more central to the well-being of the river.

In many instances sportfishing is key to ecological initiatives, and the money it provides goes a long way toward preserving a pristine environment. We have highlighted several examples in South America especially where the income from anglers serves to protect the rain forest and the vulnerable creatures that live in it. However, when planning your trip, always check local regulations and double-check fishing methods and closed seasons. These central fishing reserves have to be treated with enormous sensitivity by the visiting angler.

How to use this book

This book is laid out geographically, highlighting 500 of the best fishing opportunities in the six most important fishing regions of the world. We have made no distinction between sea and freshwater fishing and the approaches are spread between bait, lure, and fly techniques. Also featured are thirty Bucket List Fish entries—iconic species on every angler's wishlist that can be fished in multiple locations. We hope, therefore, that we have included an adventure for everyone, wherever they might live or travel to.

The criteria we used to choose the fishing opportunities and species are simple. We looked at fish that are interesting, exciting, and offer thrilling sporting challenges. But always do your research. Check for what are regarded as sport fish and what as invasive species in the area you are going to visit. We hope to have covered major fishing expeditions that will demand real research and effort to undertake, along with ideas for the vacation angler to enjoy in a casual afternoon. We have tried to emphasize the importance of conservation and have not included fish that are on red lists of threatened species or are considered dangerous. But rules and restrictions change rapidly, and climatic and political changes can also affect accessibility and safety, so checking for updates before you travel is essential.

We hope all the entry headings stimulate your interest but the write-ups make it clear that there are great differences in the level of difficulty involved. If you are a novice angler and unsure of your abilities it makes sense to avoid the more serious expeditions—for now at least! Whether you are experienced or not, we cannot overemphasize the importance guides make on most angling experiences. The vast majority of guides are knowledgeable, conscientious, and will bend over backward to bring you success and keep you safe.

Below | Research your dream trip and you may be on your way to catching a sailfish

The importance of planning

The entries in this book will hopefully inspire you to start planning your own angling adventures but it would be irresponsible not to add some cold words of advice at this point. Here goes and apologies if some tips sound obvious but you'd be surprised how even the obvious can be overlooked . . .

- Ensure you have a waterproof poncho and thermals if you suspect it will get cold.

- A roll of gaffer tape can wrap rod tubes, patch up split luggage, or coil round a flashlight so you can hold it in your teeth. A good knife and sharp scissors can be a godsend in the wild. A trusty whistle can save your life if you are out in no-man's-land too. Remember to take your medications along.

- Take every scrap of fishing gear you could ever need if you are traveling out of reach of civilization; there are many places where the nearest tackle shop is a thousand miles away or more.

- Take care physically. Watch your step, you don't want a broken ankle in the jungle.

- Be patient at airports and in camps with guides who come from different cultures with looser schedules and unknown timetables. Learn to trust your guide and realize you can't control everything in an alien environment. Be brave but not gung ho.

- Finally, prepare as well as you possibly can, especially when it comes to timings. Monsoons, wet and dry seasons, early snow falls, late springs, and all the rest of these meteorological mysteries can really mess up your trip, especially in the modern era of climate change.

That's the dull stuff done with! Now, go and fish and live the angling adventures of your dreams.

JOHN BAILEY

NORTH AMERICA

HAWAII

NORTH AMERICA: ENTRY LIST

1 Tuckamore River, Newfoundland	43 Trinity River, Texas
2 Miramichi River, New Brunswick	44 Trinity River, Texas
3 B3 Beat, Bonaventure River,	45 Trinity River, Texas
Gaspé Peninsula, Quebec	46 Livingston Dam, Trinity River,
4 St. Lawrence Seaway, Quebec	Texas
5 Amethyst Lake, Alberta	47 Topock Gorge, Colorado River,
6 Harrison River, British Columbia	Arizona/California
7 Harrison River, British Columbia	48 Green River, Utah
8 Nicomen Slough, British Columbia	49 Lake Mead, Las Vegas, Nevada
9 Fraser River, British Columbia	50 California
10 Fraser River, British Columbia	51 Pacific Coast, San Diego, California
11 Skeena River, British Columbia	52 Ko Olina, Oahu, Hawaii
12 Campbell River, Discovery Passage,	53 Kona, Big Island, Hawaii
Vancouver Island, British	54 Lake Wilson (Wahiawa Reservoir),
Columbia	Oahu Island, Hawaii
13 Ucluelet, Vancouver Island,	55 Hawaii
British Columbia	56 Maalaea Harbor, Maui Island,
14 Coghlan Lake, Yukon	Hawaii
15 Drury Lake, Yukon	57 Port Allen, Kauai Island, Hawaii
16 Hidden Lakes, Yukon	58 Kauai, Hawaii
17 Whitehorse, Yukon	59 Puget Sound, Seattle, Washington
18 Moosehead Lake, Maine	60 Snake River, Hells Canyon,
19 Lake Champlain, Vermont	Washington
20 Cape Cod, Massachusetts	61 Bristol Bay, Alaska
21 Montauk Point, Long Island,	62 Homer, Alaska
New York State	63 Alaska
22 Salmon River, Lake Ontario,	64 Kasilof River, Anchorage, Alaska
New York State	65 Kenai River/Ship Creek,
23 New York City Harbor,	Anchorage, Alaska
New York City	66 Naknek Lake, Katmai National Park
24 Norfolk Canyon, Virginia	and Preserve, Alaska
25 The Outer Banks, North Carolina	67 Deshka River, Alaska
26 Charleston, South Carolina	68 Flathead River, Montana
27 Boca Grande, Florida	69 Fort Peck Lake, Montana
28 Everglades National Park, Florida	70 Madison River, Montana
29 Destin Harbor, Florida	71 Bighorn River, Montana/Wyoming
30 Islamorada, Florida Keys	72 Devils Lake, North Dakota
31 Islamorada, Florida Keys	73 Cheyenne River/Lake Oahe,
32 Florida Bay, Islamorada,	South Dakota
Florida Keys	74 Lake Vermillion, Minnesota
33 Florida Bay, Islamorada,	75 Beaver Island, Lake Michigan
Florida Keys	76 Lake St. Clair, Detroit, Michigan
34 Islamorada, Florida Keys	77 Lake Aguamilpa, Mexico
35 Islamadora, Florida Keys	78 Acapulco, Guerrero, Mexico
36 Islamadora, Florida Keys	79 Barra De Navidad, Costalegre,
37 Key Largo to Key West, Florida	Jalisco, Mexico
38 Henderson Swamp, Baton Rouge,	80 Lake El Salto, Mazatlán, Sinaloa,
Louisiana	Mexico
39 Matagorda Bay, Texas City Coast,	81 Lake Baccarac, Sinaloa, Mexico
Galveston	82 Mazatlán, Sinaloa, Mexico
40 Galveston Beach, Texas	83 Los Cabos, Baja, Mexico
41 Matagorda Bay, Texas	84 Isla Blanca, Mexico
42 Texas City Pier, Texas	

1
An Atlantic romance
Tuckamore River, Newfoundland
June to September
Atlantic salmon

There's a romance to fishing here, and any visitor would do well to follow the words of Newfoundland poet Edwin John Pratt and "heed the sea's strong voice." There's nowhere better than just south of Hare Bay Islands Ecological Reserve in the finger of land that pokes out into the North Atlantic. Here, Atlantic salmon run in the Tuckamore River (July and August are the most productive months) and offer incredible sport on the dry fly. Fish often hold close to the bank, so that's the place to start.

2
Stripers on the fly
Miramichi River, New Brunswick
May and early June
Striped bass

At times, the Miramichi can seem alive with bass. Some anglers joke that during spawning, when males thrash around the females on the surface, you can walk across the river on their backs. For the bigger fish, seek out the deeper channels and use oversized flies with a sinking line on a 10 wt rod. While most bass from the Miramichi are young males under 2 ft (0.6 m) long, this method can produce much bigger fish.

2 | **The Miramichi River runs through thick forests**

3 | **The Bonaventure River is famed for its clarity**

3
Salmon by design

B3 Beat, Bonaventure River, Gaspé Peninsula,
Quebec
June to end of September
Atlantic salmon

There are stretches of the Bonaventure
River, as it twists and turns through the
countryside, that look as if they have been
designed for catching salmon. The number
of fish, clarity of the water—visibility on this
beat can be 100 ft (30 m) or more—and
sheer joy of the surroundings will take your
breath away. At times you may have to fish
between kayaks, but this is more than
compensated for by the wonders that
live in this river.

4
Hard-fighting river carp

St. Lawrence Seaway, Quebec
May to June
Common carp

The Seaway System is part of a marine
highway around 2,300 mi (3,701 km) long
that stretches from the Atlantic all the way
to Lake Ontario in the Great Lakes, and
beyond. Since it opened in 1959, it's
estimated that over 2.75 billion tons (2.5
billion tonnes) of cargo have been moved
through these waters. Fortunately, there's
also plenty of room for a large population of
common carp, heavy from the nutrient-rich
environment, but muscular from swimming
against the strong currents.

5
Worms for big walleyes
Amethyst Lake, Alberta
Spring to summer
Walleye

Almost at the point where Alberta nudges into British Columbia, sits Amethyst Lake, at the foot of the Rampart Range. There are backcountry lodges galore and plenty of campgrounds, but this is caribou country, so no dogs are allowed. Ice is usually off the lake by July 1, so rise early and start in the shallows until the sun comes up; then follow the walleye into deeper water. Live bait—minnows, worms, and leeches—are a good choice and be prepared for a fight because even small ones scrap like crazy.

6
King of the river
Harrison River, British Columbia
July to September
King salmon (chinook)

Far up the clear water of Harrison River, there are deep pools where the male chinook make their final stand against each other to get into position to spawn. They are ready to attack anything even remotely resembling a threat to their territory. That's why it's best to use a noisy bait, like a rattling deep-diving lure. Many chinooks caught weigh between 20 and 30 lb (9 and 13 kg) with some 50 lb (22.5 kg) plus.

5 | **Amethyst Lake is one of the great walleye waters**

7 | **A "pink" battles for its freedom**

8 | **A chinook salmon is gently returned to the river**

7
Pink salmon and pink flies

Harrison River, British Columbia

Odd years only, September to November

Pink salmon (humpback salmon)

Harrison River is a tributary to the much larger Fraser River in British Columbia, where many species of Pacific salmon make their last and only spawning runs. The Harrison is narrower than Fraser River, but just as impressive with mountains, lush green banks, and crystal-clear water. The reason for the pink salmon species' special two-year appearance is due to the fact that the pinks migrate to the sea the same year they are born and return to the rivers 18 months later. They are normally caught from 4.5 to 12 lb (2 to 5.5 kg), and up to 15 lb (6.8 kg). The pinks are caught on lures, spoons, and pink, fluffy wet-flies.

8
Silverware of the finest quality

Nicomen Slough, British Columbia

April to November

Chinook salmon

The Nicomen Slough runs parallel, and into, the Fraser. It is not much different from the other rivers in the area, but for some reason coho are plentiful here during their spawning run. The chinook salmon is a one-off. It doesn't develop into a toothy jawed fish, like its Pacific salmon brethren, but remains sleek and pretty; this, and the fact that it is considered to be the best-tasting salmon in the system, puts it top of the local target-list. It does not grow that big, but what it lacks in size it makes up for in tenacity; it is reckoned to be the wildest fighting of the Pacific salmon, making long runs, and jumping spectacularly.

Bald eagles scavenge the banks of the river

The white sturgeon is the catch of a lifetime

The sheer scale of the Fraser River will take your breath away

9
Great whites
Fraser River, British Columbia
September and October
White sturgeon

The Fraser is the longest river in British Columbia. It runs from the Rocky Mountains to the Pacific, through some of the most beautiful, mountainous areas that Canada offers; also home to amazing fauna such as bears, bald eagles, and deer. The white sturgeon lives much of its life in the Pacific, but migrates to the big rivers of North America to reproduce. Aside from growing very big, these beautiful great white sturgeon fight like few other fish, launching themselves into the air—even the biggest ones—and hurling forward like an express train. They are fished on the bottom with heavy sinkers to keep the bit steady in the strong current, and the baits to use are bagged salmon roe, salmon belly meat, eulachon or oilfish (a species of smelt), lamprey pieces, or, on desperate days, stinky bait such as rotten salmon.

10
The dog run
Fraser River, British Columbia
September to December
Chum salmon (dog salmon)

Sunrise over the Fraser River on a foggy morning is breathtaking, as the outlines of the mountains are revealed. The spawning male salmon turn brownish and develop a crooked mouth and large teeth, which is why they're called "dogs." They are normally caught from 10 to 13 lb (4.5 to 6 kg), and up to 35 lb (16 kg). Chum are caught on lures, spoons, and fluffy wet-flies, and considered one of the best fighting Pacific salmons.

11
Silver from the sea
Skeena River, British Columbia
February to October
Steelhead

The mighty, legendary Skeena River is regarded by some as the last, and certainly the greatest, bastion of North American steelhead. In part this is because there are no large dams to impede spawning runs, nor hatcheries to dilute the native stock, or salmon farms to pollute the habitat. There is low human density in the river catchment and sensitive forest management. Fishing, too, is catch and release with single barbless flies.

11 | **A steelhead caught on the Skeena River**

12
A thousand colors and shapes
Campbell River, Discovery Passage, Vancouver
Island, British Columbia
All year
Pacific salmon

When the angler, conservationist, and
author Roderick Haig-Brown wrote: "I
have never seen a river that I could not
love. Moving water . . . has a thousand
colors and a thousand shapes, yet it follows
laws so definite that the tiniest streamlet
is an exact replica of a great river," he was
almost certainly thinking of the Campbell.
At the mouth of the river, you will find all
five sub-species of Pacific salmon, which
is why it is known as the "salmon capital
of the world."

13
Salmon of the storm
Ucluelet, Vancouver Island, British Columbia
July to August
Pacific salmon

This peninsula has more than enough to
offer; there's all-year surfing, whale watching,
kayaking, hiking in one of the three regions
that make up the Pacific Rim National Park
Reserve, and then there's storm-watching.
From October low pressure moves in, with
winds of up to 43 mph (70 km/h) chasing
its tail, resulting in the perfect conditions
to watch as 25 ft (7.6 m) waves crash upon
the shore. It's why Ucluelet means "people
of the safe harbor" in the Indigenous
Nuu-chah-nulth language. And if you can
drag yourself away from all that, the salmon-
fishing is superb.

12 | **The Campbell is home to all five Pacific salmon species**

15 | **Grayling fight with every last ounce of strength**

14
Pike in crystal-clear water
Coghlan Lake, Yukon
May to September
Northern pike

Famed for its unparalleled acceleration
power, the northern pike is the epitome of
a fish that won't come quietly. At Coghlan
Lake—said to have the clearest water in the
Yukon—the pike have grown to 30 lb (13 kg)
plus by dining on grayling, whitefish, and
burbot, but they're not averse to large
spoons and spinners. If you're not fishing
with a guide, try the edges of weed beds or
where shoals drop off into deeper water.

15
On top of the world with monster grayling
Drury Lake, Yukon
June to July
Arctic grayling

At nearly 2,500 ft (762 m) above sea level,
Drury Lake is well worth the plane ride for
anyone who wants to feel the joy of a large
bag of beautiful, but pocket-sized grayling.
In this remote 15 mi (24 km) long lake,
surrounded by the Pelly Mountains, the
"sailfish of the north" grows to a whopping
4 lb (1.8 kg) and then some. Spinners and
spoons will account for larger specimens but
for real fun, use a fly-rod. Oh, and take
binoculars; the wildlife is spectacular.

16
Rainbows from the wilderness

Hidden Lakes, Yukon
June to October
Rainbow trout

Part of the protected Greenbelt Park Reserve, this feels like wilderness without being much more than a ten-minute car drive from Whitehorse, Yukon's capital city.

The collection of "kettle lakes"—formed from depressions left behind after the last ice age—are home to large numbers of stocked rainbow trout. Stock-fish are bred in hatcheries in Whitehorse and then trucked to the lakes at the end of May. Dry fly-fishing from the shore works well here, and fish will often compete to snatch a well-presented surface-fly.

16 | **Catch the aurora borealis over Hidden Lake**

17 | **Dotted markings of the lake trout**

18 | **Ice fishing for trout with a palm rod**

17
Yukon's midnight trout
Whitehorse, Yukon
May to July
Lake trout

Yukon's capital city Whitehorse, with a population of just 28,000, makes the perfect base for anglers in search of lake trout. Found in most still waters in the Yukon, lake trout are the largest of the freshwater char family and are highly prized for their glorious markings and salmon-pink fin-tips. After ice-out you'll find them in the shallows, but come July they drift into deeper water and your best bet is a heavy jig or spoon. In summer, thanks to the midnight sun, you can fish for them all night long.

18
Drilling for trout
Moosehead Lake, Maine
Jan 1 to April 30
Lake trout, brook trout

Once a working-lake with dozens of steamboats ferrying supplies and workers to and from the many lumber camps in the area, Maine's largest lake is now a magnet for that special breed of angler who enjoys a style of fishing quite unlike any other—ice fishing. Along with spud-bars for measuring ice depth, augurs for drilling holes, and skimmers for ladling out the slush, many anglers also take portable shelters with propane heaters inside and use "rods" that are 2 ft (60 cm) long or less (so-called "palm rods" that look like a conductor's baton).

21 | **The haunting beauty of Montauk Point**

19
Monsters of the deep

Lake Champlain, Vermont
Late spring to early summer
Perch, salmon, northern pike

Anglers in search of monsters could do worse than visit Lake Champlain, said to be the home of Vermont's very own Loch Ness Monster. The beastie in question is actually Gitaskog (gee-tah-skog) a horned sea-serpent that features commonly in the mythology of the Algonquin. Subject of a truly terrible (as opposed to terrifying) horror movie of the same name, it is said to resemble a seahorse. Those of a less superstitious nature can always stick to the real monsters—salmon, perch, and pike.

20
Fishing steeped in history

Cape Cod, Massachusetts
May to July
Striped bass, bluefin tuna

Although they settled on the mainland in Plymouth, the Pilgrims first fetched up at Provincetown, on the tip of the beautiful crook of land that seems to say "come hither" to the entire Atlantic Ocean. Since then, Cape Cod has preserved its premier place in the nation's history books—it's also home to America's oldest library—and has become popular with holiday-seekers; it was JFK's favorite vacation destination. Charter trips usually start with tuna in the morning before moving on to striped bass in the afternoon.

21
Navigating dangerous waters

Montauk Point, Long Island, New York State
December to April for cod; June to September for shark; July to September for tuna
Bluefin tuna, cod, shark

Looking north to the Montauk Point Lighthouse, it is said that if the night is dark enough and the angler patient enough, you can see a tiny light—a ghostly candle borne by the spirit of a young woman who drowned off Long Island. Fortunately, charter services ply their trade here, so today's angler can relax and enjoy the fishing—whether for a 40 lb (18 kg) cod, a 200 lb (90 kg) mako shark, or a 1,000 lb (454 kg) bluefin tuna.

22
Plenty of fish, not much elbow room
Salmon River, Lake Ontario, New York State
Late August to October
King salmon, sockeye salmon

The annual salmon-run on the aptly-named Salmon River in upstate New York attracts thousands of anglers every year. Although it can be crowded, the size and quality of the fish more than makes up for the occasional bit of overcrowding. Most methods work well on this 17 mi (27 km) stretch, but bigger fish often come out to clumps of trout eggs (about the size of a strawberry) tied in special mesh-bags and then attached to the hook. These are fished under floats in the deep runs and holes where the fish congregate.

22 | **Salmon River gets plenty of angler attention**

23 | Urban environments can offer great fishing

23
Big Apple fishing

New York City Harbor, New York City
All year, May for striped bass
Striped bass

Under the New York City-skyline, in the big harbor area, there is surprisingly good fishing. Various kinds of charters are available, from small specialist boats, to larger family-trip or group boats, that can supply all tackle if you so desire. There are many different species to catch for any type of angler. On the group charters you will mainly catch bottom-fish like black sea bass, striped searobin "rabbitfish," northern puffer "blowfish," flounder, or "fluke," and many other species. The highlight for the local anglers is when the striped bass are around in May; an incredibly popular fish all along the US east coast.

24
Discover the other Grand Canyon
Norfolk Canyon, Virginia
June to September for billfish, June to November for tuna
Billfish, tuna

Around 35 mi (56 km) off the shore of the eastern United States, from Virginia right up to Maine, the continental shelf is fissured by a series of mighty canyons—thirteen in all—hundreds of feet deep. One of these— the Norfolk Canyon—is an echo of some ancient river that ran 15,000 years ago, when this was dry land. The canyon is now a fertile hunting-ground for billfish—especially marlin—and yellowfin tuna.

25
Hunting the wolves of the sea
The Outer Banks, North Carolina
Late spring to early fall
Marlin, sailfish

This 200 mi (322 km) long necklace of islands strung along the North Carolina coast is home to some of the most spectacular fishing in North America. Predicting when marlin season will peak is complicated by seasonal storms, but September is often the best month. Initially fish are located by sight—feeding birds are a giveaway—and then confirmed via sonar. Marlin are solitary predators while sailfish hunt in packs, hence their nickname, the "wolves of the sea."

26
Say a little prayer . . .
Charleston, South Carolina
Spring to fall for barracuda; July to August for sailfish; November to March for wahoo
Barracuda, sailfish, and wahoo

Anglers praying for good luck are spoiled for choice in the "holy city," so-called because of the 400-plus church-steeples that pepper the skyline. Inshore it's mainly barracuda that attract anglers here, and they give great sport on lures of small dead-baits. Offshore, it's wahoo and the sailfish, which can reach speeds of 70 mph (113 km/h).

25 | **Shore fishing in North Carolina**

27 | **A magnificent tarpon comes to the boat**

28 | **An endless variety of scenery . . . and alligators**

27
Looking for the "silver king"
Boca Grande, Florida
April to August
Tarpon

Having begun life as a fishing village, it's fitting that the now exclusive island of Boca Grande is still making at least a partial living from the sea. As the tarpon capital of the world, however, the emphasis is not on subsistence, but rather on sportfishing. Tarpon is an ancient fish—fossils have been found that date back 125 million years—that abounds in these waters from spring to summer and there are plenty of guides who can take anglers to the best inshore or offshore fishing grounds.

28
Fish with the alligators
Everglades National Park, Florida
April to August
Common snook

The Everglades lies a boat-ride from the Florida Keys. Mostly known for its alligators and mosquitoes, it is often bypassed by anglers, but from shore-side, you get the best of several worlds; it is beautiful, green, and exciting; there are many fish; and you are not all that bothered by pesky mosquitos. Along the outskirts of the Everglades another of Florida's top fish—the snook—is found in big numbers. It is revered for its pugnacity, as well as the ferocity with which it attacks its prey, and thereby anglers' baits.

29 | Sunset and sunrise usually see the best sport

30 | Use every method to catch these shark

29
Better to be lucky . . .
Destin Harbor, Florida
May to October
King mackerel

All anglers can testify to the importance of
luck, indeed the author H.T. Sheringham
wrote: "For myself, I take my stand entirely
on luck. To the novice I would say: 'Cultivate
your luck. Prop it up with omens and signs
of good purport. Watch for magpies on
your path . . . Be on friendly terms with
a black cat.'" The great man would have
appreciated the attractions of Destin Harbor,
an archetypal Florida marina and dubbed
"the world's luckiest fishing village" thanks
to the range of species and their seeming
eagerness to take a bait.

30
Catch Florida's sociable shark
Islamorada, Florida Keys
Spring to fall
Bonnethead shark

Viewers of the hit TV-show *Bloodline* starring
Sissy Spacek and Sam Shepherd will already
be familiar with the sunlit wonder that is
Islamorada—a village across six islands,
nestled in the Florida Keys. Bonnethead
sharks (affectionately known as
"shovelheads") are sociable creatures and
prowl the shallow waters here in abundance,
usually in small schools of up to fifteen fish.
A shark with a partly plant-based diet, it will
fall to jigs, flies, spinners, and fresh bait—
especially crab and shrimp.

31
World class
Islamorada, Florida Keys
April to August
Atlantic tarpon

Florida Keys is a 15.5 mi (25 km) long archipelago of coral islands with palm trees, and waters filled with exciting and exotic fish. This is probably the best place in the world to catch one of the most coveted fish of all, the tarpon. The tarpon thrive on fish and swimming crabs which they can find in between the islands (keys), but most often under bridges. The tarpon encapsulates the essence of exotic sportfishing: big, beautiful, warm-water fish, hard fighting, and jumping free of the water. It can be caught on lures, natural baits, and on a fly.

31 | In warm waters, this is the ultimate target

32
Many species with many teeth
Florida Bay, Islamorada, Florida Keys
April to August
Sharks

The views of the Florida Keys from the adjacent Florida Bay are spectacular with green land, blue water, and blue skies. This is where many exciting shark species roam: from the huge and dangerous hammerhead sharks, tiger sharks, and bull sharks, to the more benign reef shark species, spinner sharks, and nurse sharks. The sharks are opportunistic fish, taking whatever food is readily available, so they are fairly easily caught on dead bait on the bottom, or under a float. While they are slow and heavy fighters—don't let that fool you. If they get near your boat, they can jump up and snap at you with dire consequences.

32 | **For shark you can't beat the Florida Keys**

33
Tabletop fish
Florida Bay, Islamorada, Florida Keys
April to August
Southern stingray

Almost everywhere in the Florida Keys and along the Everglades, the waters are exotic and beautiful—as long as you avoid hurricane season. You can catch the ravenous southern stingray here using natural bait, and nothing compares to fighting this fish; first it tries to "suck" itself to the bottom, requiring concerted effort to extract, and then you fight what resembles a big oak tabletop, skirting around in the water. It's tiring, but worth the agony when you land this beautiful creature.

34
Flats fighters
Islamorada, Florida Keys
February to April and June to July
Permit, bonefish, bonnethead

The flats around Florida Keys are world-famous for bonefish and permit. The fish here are easily spooked, so stealth is key, along with precision casting. Use light tackle and they will give you an unrivaled battle for their size. Sometimes you get a side-catch in the form of bonnethead, or bonnet sharks, which stalk the shallows for easy prey. Permit and bonefish are usually caught on live crab, shrimps, and flies.

35
Sharp-toothed angling appetizers
Islamorada, Florida Keys
Spring and summer
Ladyfish

A curious tale this, of a silver fish, most often used as bait for bigger species that nevertheless has become a brilliant "angling appetizer" thanks to its razor-sharp teeth and habit of hurling itself out of the water when hooked; and unlike many uniformly smaller baitfish, there's always the chance of getting a double figure Ladyfish just when you least expect it. Happy in brackish lagoons and mangroves, the Ladyfish will also wander several miles offshore, and although watching one jump is a memorable sight, be careful—that's usually the moment when they throw the hook.

36
A delightful and delicious snapper
Islamorada, Florida Keys
Winter to spring
Mutton snapper

Little mutton snapper are delicate, coral-colored cuties with beautiful multicolored markings under the eyes, and tiny scales like chainmail. As they get larger and older, the features of big mutton snappers—a bit like humans—become exaggerated, and they acquire huge heads and massive, disgruntled-looking mouths; if they had ears, they would be enormous. One of the best ways to catch them off the Keys is to use a live ballyhoo (a small baitfish) and float it along the bottom of the reef. Mutton snapper are also delicious—try baking them wrapped in foil with herb-butter and lemon.

35–36 | **The Islamorada Coast is all about drama: dramatic fish, dramatic fishing, and dramatic weather**

37
Southern street-fighters

Key Largo to Key West, Florida
March to April
Yellowfin tuna, amberjack

The Florida Keys have history—the
modern, gritty kind of history that
inspired Ernest Hemingway to write: "It's
the best place I've ever been, anytime,
anywhere. Flowers, tamarind trees, guava
trees, coconut palms . . . Got tight last
night on absinthe and did knife tricks."
The fishing is similarly visceral, especially
with a large amberjack on the other end
of the line. The Marathon Hump—
basically an underwater mountain—is a
favored mark because its proximity to the
Gulf Stream attracts small fish, which in
turn attracts bigger fish.

38
Unearth a living fossil

Henderson Swamp, Baton Rouge, Louisiana
July to August
Alligator gar

Memorably described by that monster-catcher-in-
chief Jeremy Wade as "a living fossil that's been
unchanged for more than 60 million years," the
alligator gar is the apex predator of the
Henderson Swamp waters. Females grow larger
than males—big ones are 250 lb (113 kg) plus,
8 ft (2.4 m) long, and powerful enough to tow a
boat—but both sexes have a distinctive double-
row of teeth along the top jaw. Like all large fish,
alligator gars need careful handling once tamed
and plenty of time to revive before being
returned to the depths from which they came.

37 | Reeling in a yellowfin tuna

The Sheepshead is great to look at and fun to catch

39
BUCKET LIST FISH: Sheepshead (sea bream)
MATAGORDA BAY, TEXAS CITY COAST, GALVESTON

Let's get this out of the way at the start: the sheepshead gets its name from the unsettling similarity between its teeth (the upper teeth particularly) and the teeth of an actual sheep. That also means its mouth strongly resembles a human mouth, complete with incisors, molars, and large grinding teeth at the back. This has caused many an "ew" moment for anglers not expecting to see fish that look as though they've swallowed a set of dentures. Visitors can enjoy catching sheepshead all along this part of the coast, all the way up to Galveston—just forget the teeth and focus on that fine, juicy white flesh.

40
Beach-side casting

Galveston Beach, Texas

Black drum best in March, all year for other species

Black drum, redfish, stingray

Galveston is a relaxed Victorian town with beautiful, old houses, great restaurants, and a beach for bathing. Anglers tend to show up late afternoon, when the bathing guests leave. As with Texas City Pier and Matagorda Bay, there are many species to target. On Galveston Beach, however, anglers most often fish beach-casting style, with heavy-grip sinkers, and pieces of mullet as bait; then watch for bites with the rods in rod holders.

40 | **Galveston Beach has it all—multiple species, super bathing, and fine dining when the fishing is over**

41 | **Natural beauty, fascinating wildlife, and a wealth of fish species make Matagorda Bay a must-fish location**

41
Wading with the wild fish
Matagorda Bay, Texas
All year
Redfish, Atlantic stingray, sheepshead, bull shark

The Gulf of Texas has many places where the fishing is very good. The great Matagorda Bay is very popular both for the fishing and for the beautiful vista of oyster reefs, pelicans, and an array of wildlife. The bay is shallow and the bottom is hard sand, so it is perfect for wade-fishing. After a short boat-ride to the outer reefs, you are in the middle of a variety of fish species, from small to big, from sea catfish to bull sharks, and tarpon. However, some of the most popular fish here are the redfish, stingray, speckled trout, and black drum, which are fished with a popper-float and a live shrimp on a small treble hook.

42
Where everybody goes to fish
Texas City Pier, Texas
Black drum best in March, all year for other species
Black drum, gafftopsail catfish, redfish, ladyfish, bass

Texas City Pier is a wonderful mix of mom and pop fishing along with their children, as well as serious sportfishers. This popular pier stretches more than 5 mi (8 km) out into the Gulf of Mexico and you can catch a variety of fish species and sizes. Besides big tarpon and sharks, the popular species are black drum, redfish, and various bass. The fishing is most often done beside your truck and cooler box, parked on the pier itself, or by boat. Baits used are often shrimp, crab, mullet, and other fish species. You can even fish at night, under the street lamps.

43
An opportunity in early spring
Trinity River, Texas
February to March
White bass

44
Catch an ultralight warrior
Trinity River, Texas
February to May, September, November
Yellow bass

Also called the sand bass or silver bass, what this fish may lack in size, it more than makes up for in numbers. These shoal-fish are best targeted from February to the end of March and this early start is one of the reasons anglers love them. For maximum sport, try using a super-light rod in conjunction with what's called a tandem rig—a couple of small jigs on a single line—and bump them along the bottom of the river. The white bass find this irresistible.

Although typically weighing less than 1 lb (0.45 kg), yellow bass are great fun to catch on ultra-light tackle. In spring, try spinning or jerking a live minnow to get them going; in summer, switch to night crawlers (also known as lobworms), but in the early morning or as evening draws in use a fly or nymph. Yellow bass prefer shallow water and love a good structure such as pilings, a bridge, or a jetty; these are always good spots to try.

43 | **Margaret Hunt Hill Bridge over Trinity River**

Watch out for raccoons and other creatures

Trinity River is gar paradise

The massive gar looks like a fish from prehistory

45
All sorts of alligators
Trinity River, Texas
Mid-March to October
Alligator gar, longnose gar

At over 620 mi (1,000 km) long, the Trinity River is the longest river in Texas and runs all the way through the state. It is an exotic beauty with overhanging trees, muddy banks, and cocoa-colored water. It is warm and humid, as you would expect, with raccoons and wild boars on the banks, and all sorts of creatures who can kill or maim you in an instant such as alligators, snapping turtles, black widow spiders, and venomous snakes. Here the gars, alongside the alligators, hunt alive and dead prey by effectively using sensory organs other than their eyes. So to catch these huge beasts you just need pieces of dead fish on a strong treble hook, and fairly heavy tackle. The gars jump completely free of the water when you fight them, as well as heading toward mangroves to escape, so you're in for an awesome fight. It is quite normal to catch alligator gars over 65 lb (30 kg), even up to 220 lb (100 kg) or more, with maximum weight over 440 lb (200 kg).

46 | **Fly, lure, or bait fishers will find that Livingstone Dam is a location of a lifetime**

46
Fishing heaven
Livingston Dam, Trinity River, Texas
All year
Blue catfish, flathead catfish, buffalo carp, paddlefish, sunfish

The Trinity River is dammed up, near the town of Livingston. This has created a special environment for anglers downstream of the dam, since many species are forced to congregate here. Such a variety of fish species at the dam encourages a similar variety of fishing styles: canoe-fishing, spin-fishing, fly-fishing, natural bait-fishing. The most popular species among the spin, fly, and canoe fishers are white bass, yellow bass, blue catfish, crappie, and sunfish. The natural bait-anglers go for smallmouth buffalo, black buffalo, flathead catfish, various suckers, and even large grass carp.

47
Striped bass from the miniature Grand Canyon
Topock Gorge, Colorado River, Arizona/ California
March to June
Striped bass

Topock Gorge is like a highway for striped bass. As temperatures rise in the spring, the bass, which have been lazing in Lake Havasu to the south, get in gear and begin to move up the river. As they do so, they aggressively seek out food, piling on weight as they slash and burn their way to spawning grounds in the north, up by Davis Dam at the southern tip of Lake Mohave. Fishing with "pencil poppers"' (wooden lures designed to mimic bait fish splashing on the surface) in shallow water is best first thing in the morning and as evening draws in, using cut-anchovy bait over chum (ground up bits of fish) can account for larger specimens.

48
Rainbows from emerald waters
Green River, Utah
May to October
Rainbow trout

Built in 1964, the Flaming Gorge dam has some unusual characteristics—notably four adjustable gates that can be raised and lowered to reach different water depths and help to keep the temperature of the river at around 50°F (10°C) from May through to October. This promotes insect (and fish) growth and creates an ideal habitat for both brown and rainbow trout, where the average fish will be about 18 in (46 cm) long. Why the name? From the top of the surrounding canyons, the river is a beautiful, emerald green.

49
Betting on big bass
Lake Mead, Las Vegas, Nevada
May to September
Striped bass, largemouth bass, smallmouth bass

Twenty-five miles (40 km) east of the strip, the Hoover dam sits across the Colorado river to the south and the vastness of Lake Mead to the north and east. Although best reached by boat, there are some good locations for shore-fishing, including Hemenway Harbor and Willow Beach fishing piers. Despite dropping water-levels in recent years, the famed striped bass are still a favorite target for anglers seeking a 35 or 40 lb (16 or 18 kg) fish; and if they're hard to find, then both small- and largemouth bass will usually oblige. Look for terns and gulls swooping down to take baitfish, and feeding bass will never be far away.

49 | A nice bass caught in vast Lake Mead

The glamorous rainbow trout is one of the super species of the fishing world and thrives on five continents

50
BUCKET LIST FISH: Rainbow trout
CALIFORNIA

The magnificent rainbow trout is native from Alaska to California and throughout northeast Asia, and has been introduced throughout Europe, South America, Australasia, and even Africa and India. It's flourished in every continent, often growing to 30 lb (13 kg) or more and providing sport for millions of fly-anglers. Steelhead are rainbows that live and feed in the sea, returning to freshwater to spawn. For many North American anglers, these are trophy fish above all others.

51
The jet-propelled shark
Pacific Coast, San Diego, California
April to November, but be sure to check local regulations
Shortfin mako shark

Although not particularly large as sharks go, its average size is about 7 ft (2.1 m), the shortfin mako shark has an unexpected trick up its sleeve—the ability to accelerate to around 40 mph (64 km/h), making it the fastest shark in the world. In fact, in its determination to chase down prey, the mako will often hurl itself clear out of the water. The seas off the San Diego coast are home to one of the world's main mako nursery grounds and the most exciting way to catch one is using a fly.

51 | The acceleration of a shortfin mako, especially hooked on fly, is a great experience

52
Not Penny's boat . . .
Ko Olina, Oahu, Hawaii
December to March
Marlin

Anglers who look back to the shore as their boat chugs out of Ko Olina and toward the rich fishing-grounds beyond may well feel a tingle of recognition at the sight of those rolling green hills and beautiful blue skies. That's because between 2004 and 2010 Oahu was the location for the supernatural, hit TV show, *Lost*. There'll be no time for polar bears and time-traveling shenanigans once the angling-action starts however, not with fish reaching 200 lb (91 kg) or more.

The magnificent backdrop to fishing Oahu

The moment lifetime marlin addicts live for

53
Monsters from the deep-blue sea

Kona, Big Island, Hawaii
All year
Tuna, swordfish, spearfish, marlin

In ancient Hawaii, "kapu" or sacred laws governed fishing and harvesting of resources. Anyone who fished outside of their designated time sought forgiveness and refuge within the Pu'uhonua or rock walls on the western coast of Kona. This is still an important ceremonial site, now also part of a national park. Fishing remains integral to Hawaiian culture, with one of the finest manta ray habitats in the world. Out in the deep-blue water is some of the most mouth-watering spearfish-, marlin-, swordfish-, and tuna-angling in these islands.

54
The psychedelic peacock bass

Lake Wilson (Wahiawa Reservoir),
Oahu Island, Hawaii
April to October
Peacock bass, largemouth bass

Built in 1904, the Wahiawa dam was constructed to irrigate the sugar-cane plantations nearby and almost instantly increased Oahu's cane output. Named for one of the lead engineers on the project—Albert Wilson—the reservoir is stocked with many species, including largemouth bass, but it's the peacocks that draw anglers here, thanks to their prodigious size and wonderful tie-dye coloration.

53 | **The manta ray inhabits the deep waters of Hawaii**   54 | **The peacock bass is a cornucopia of colors**

A sight to thrill any angler is the tailwalking swordfish, the acrobat of the tropical seas

55
BUCKET LIST FISH: Swordfish
HAWAII

For many top anglers, swordfish is the perfect big-game fish. It is uniquely adaptable and lives in both the tropical and temperate zones of the Atlantic, Pacific, and Indian Oceans so can be located pretty much worldwide. In Hawaii, top fishing takes place between January and May. While they can reside and feed at huge depths, they spend much of their time at the surface where they can be taken when trolling. And once hooked, the most dramatic of all blue-water fishing begins. Swordfish are the fastest fish in the sea, bar marlin, so expect searing, unstoppable runs. They are born acrobats and no other fish spends as much of the fight tail-walking, creating unforgettable images. Add in their colors, shape, and size and you have one of the world's favorites.

56
It's a fish-eat-fish world
Maalaea Harbor, Maui Island, Hawaii
March to September
Marlin, tuna, giant trevally, barracuda

The fishing here is something special, with a wide range of species and large specimens. But there's nothing quite like seeing a group of giant trevally (GT) tearing into a school of smaller fish. They circle the baitfish, driving them toward a barrier until there's no way out, and then accelerate in concert—like wolves—to attack. The small fish hurl themselves out of the sea, sometimes even onto dry land, to escape. Then again, anglers have reported reeling in a GT only to have it torn in half by an even bigger barracuda.

58
Fish from the garden island
Kauai, Hawaii
All year, apart from December through March
Mullet, red snapper

With over 95 percent of its land mass covered in pristine rain forests and mountains, it's no wonder that Kauai is called "the garden island." It's home to the 3,000 ft (900 m) deep Waimea Canyon which is the setting for Hollywood blockbusters from *Pirates of the Caribbean: On Stranger Shores* to *South Pacific*. The seas here teem with mullet and red snapper and, to maintain sustainability, there are rules visiting anglers must adhere to regarding licenses, when fishing is permitted, fish sizes, and limits. Once those are sorted, the island offers stunning shore-fishing against a picture-postcard backdrop.

57
Big game fishing, fighting talk
Port Allen, Kauai Island, Hawaii
All year
Sailfish, swordfish, tuna

When it comes to using a fighting-chair—the piece of specialized equipment that will help stop a 500 lb (226 kg) monster from pulling you into the ocean—there are techniques and etiquette to learn. First, you fight the fish with the rod not the reel; using the reel like a winch will exhaust the angler quickly, so it's important to use the rod as the lever to pull the fish toward the boat. Need to bring in lots of line fast? Place one foot on the deck, leave the other on the footstool, lean forward so your winding shoulder is over the reel, and wind from there. Fish gone deep? Try and time the rise and fall of the ocean swell so that it helps as the fish is being pumped. And the etiquette? Don't sit in the seat before a fish is hooked. It's bad luck.

59 | **Puget Sound is known for chinook and orca**

60 | **Snake River sturgeon offer a unique experience**

59
Healthy competition
Puget Sound, Seattle, Washington
June to August
Chinook salmon

Visitors to Puget Sound—a remarkable coastal region that encompasses busy freight ports, the city of Seattle, several river estuaries, as well as fertile farmland—have some serious competition when it comes to chasing the Chinook salmon for which the sound is rightly famed. This comes in the form of the J, K, and L pods, three groups of orcas—known as the "Southern Residents"—which feed almost exclusively on Chinooks. Best to keep out of their way, eh?

60
Dinosaurs of the deep
Snake River, Hells Canyon, Washington
Spring
White sturgeon

Catching a white sturgeon will represent the pinnacle for many—their huge size, terrifying power, and the sense of an ancient creature somehow frozen in time is enough to reduce the most experienced angler to a quivering wreck. Add a natural wonder such as Hells Canyon as a backdrop (hewn from a plateau by the Snake River over millions of years) and the scene is set for the experience of an angling lifetime. Although fish move constantly in early spring, Heller Bar is always a good bet.

61 | **Bristol Bay is a great location for sockeye and coho**

62 | **A giant halibut is levered from the depths**

61
The salmon supermarket
Bristol Bay, Alaska
June to July
Sockeye salmon, coho salmon, king salmon

When it comes to salmon, the Bristol Bay ecosystem stands head and shoulders above the rest—one of the reasons it's known as "America's fish basket." It's home to the largest sockeye salmon runs in the world (just under 50 percent of the total wild sockeye catch). In recent years the area has battled to prevent a massive open-pit mine from being developed at the headwaters to the bay. While conservationists have been successful so far, developers show few signs of backing off, so enjoy these gorgeous, productive waters while there's still time.

62
Halibut heaven
Homer, Alaska
May to September
Halibut

Homer is a haven for anglers who love to catch the largest flatfish in the sea. These omnivores can grow to 8 ft (2.4 m) long and weigh up to 500 lb (226 kg) and because they live on the ocean floor they need a lot of winding to bring up to the surface; hooking a really big one is a bit like reeling in a baby grand piano. Giant flatfish abound in the ocean here, which is why it's known as the "halibut capital of the world."

A chum salmon is one of the largest species of Pacific salmon

63
BUCKET LIST FISH: Pacific salmon
ALASKA

A truly super group of salmon species including the pink, the coho, the chum, the sockeye, and the chinook that run the rivers from Alaska to California, and those in the extreme northeast of Asia. Chinook grows huge, over 100 lb (45 kg), and the sockeye male glows vivid crimson at spawning time, but all these salmon are magnificent creatures. They have provided food for bears, seals, and hunters over eons and now provide sport for anglers. What a privilege to cast a line for these natural wonders.

64
Salmon from the Kenai's less famous cousin
Kasilof River, Anchorage, Alaska
Spring to fall
Pacific salmon

Smaller than, and not as well known as, the Kenai River, the Kasilof starts at the Tustumena Lake and then runs fast and glacial into the Cook inlet. While there are some spots to fish from the banks, visiting anglers mainly use guided drift boats (there's a section of the river designated "drift-only") to get right on top of the fish. Sockeye, king, silver, and pink salmon can be caught on the fly or by spinning, trolling, or fishing a bait such as trout eggs under a float.

65
You're looking swell, Dolly
Kenai River/Ship Creek, Anchorage, Alaska
May to September
King salmon, sockeye salmon, coho salmon, rainbow trout, Dolly Varden

Whether it's Ship Creek, which wends its way through northern Anchorage itself, or the wilder Kenai River to the south, famed for its aquamarine water, this has to be a salmon angler's bucket-list destination. The Kenai has ten separate salmon runs, making it a tremendous fishery for fly-fishing, trolling, or lure-casting. The most distinctive fish here is the Dolly Varden, a char named for its colorful spotted belly that echoes a nineteenth-century dress pattern.

66
Fishing with bears
Naknek Lake, Katmai National Park and Preserve, Alaska
June to July
King salmon, sockeye salmon

Naknek Lake and its river-system support a large population of salmon and compared with many Alaskan lakes it's relatively easy to get there. Although it's estimated that the area gets around 30,000 visitors a year (many carrying fishing rods), the main competition around here are the brown bears who love the king and sockeye salmon.

67
Mega salmon in the forest
Deshka River, Alaska
April to November
Chinook salmon (king salmon)

Here in the forest you have black bears and giant moose for company. The chinook is a beast. Some king salmon don't migrate; they remain in the rivers, feed primarily on roe, and are normally caught from 11 to 65 lb (5 to 30 kg), up to a whopping 130 lb (60 kg) plus. They are usually caught on a large, single hook with a small bag of salmon roe attached, or with rattling lures.

68
Cutthroat fishing in America
Flathead River, Montana
April to September
Westslope cutthroat trout

So-called because of the red "gash" under its bottom jaw, the westslope cutthroat trout is the state-fish of Montana and found in plentiful numbers throughout the Flathead river-system. Drawing experienced anglers and beginners alike, the Middle Fork of the river is particularly suited to the novice thanks to long stretches of slow, placid glides. Book a day's drift-boat fishing—some newcomers catch a fish on the fly even as they're learning to cast.

69
Plenty of fish, not many anglers
Fort Peck Lake, Montana
Late May to early June for pike, fall for trout
Lake trout, northern pike

Fort Peck lake offers the perfect combination of large fish and not many people fishing for them. Adventurous anglers come here for the solitude, lake trout, and northern pike. The fish are polar opposites; while the trout are turbo-charged and aggressive, the pike are lazy, especially after spawning. The best chance of catching a big one is to find deeper water near their spawning bays, then work a 6 to 10 in (15 to 25 cm) lure at different depths.

68 | **Spring to fall sport on the Flathead River**   69 | **You'll love the solitude of Fort Peck Lake**

70
Still worth it, despite the crowds

Madison River, Montana

Late April to September

Rainbow trout

In 1914, Edward Ringwood Hewitt, author, angler, and pioneer of underwater photography, recorded a visit to the Madison river in a diary entry that reads: "When we returned to the [Old Faithful] Inn we laid out both catches on the ground and I found I had been beaten. He had 165 and I had 162." It says something of the fecundity of the Madison that despite its ongoing popularity—anglers swarm here during the season—it remains a prolific water for rainbow trout, especially for the early riser or those prepared to fish into the evening.

71
Where the trout fishing is hot

Bighorn River, Montana/Wyoming

May to June

Brown trout

Most anglers are drawn to the stretch of river below the Yellowtail Dam, home to a large population of wild brown trout—estimates say between 3,000 to 5,000 fish per mile— where the rich aquatic life has allowed them to prosper and grow to an average of 15 in (38 cm) long. But venture upstream into Wyoming, and at Thermopolis there are way fewer anglers, but just as many trout. Those who tire of landing big brownies can adjourn to the nearby Hot Springs State Park for a relaxing dip before returning to the fray.

70 | **The Madison River is a rainbow trout mecca**

72
Way down in the hole
Devils Lake, North Dakota
Late summer to late fall
Perch

This is such a large area of water (281 sq mi; 728 sq km) that it's hard to know where to start. Fortunately, there are knowledgeable locals, helpful tackle shops, and plenty of fish. Ice-fishing is something else, and the way a frozen lake is reduced to a tiny hole—like a gunsight down to the fish—makes for a unique experience. The perch here are eager to bite on shrimp, lobworms, maggots, or a tungsten jig. Sunny, stable conditions are best. Dress for the weather.

73
Find salmon in the wilderness
Cheyenne River/Lake Oahe, South Dakota
Spring to summer
Pacific salmon

Where the Cheyenne River meets the Missouri River in Lake Oahe, Pacific salmon gorge themselves on shoals of rainbow smelt—baitfish that grow to about 10 in (25 cm) long. Using lures which mimic the smelt it's possible to catch plenty of salmon, though anglers with access to a boat will do best. The lake's 2,250 mi (3,621 km) shoreline is largely undeveloped and draws campers, swimmers, hunters, and hikers. Fortunately there's plenty of space for all.

74
Garish lures for giant fish
Lake Vermillion, Minnesota
Spring to fall
Muskellunge

To grab the attention of one of the behemoth muskellunge (known as muskies) here, you need a lure that will stand out from the crowd. The anglers targeting the big ones use massive lures—imagine a large zucchini—brightly colored, with iridescent bits and bobs, and treble hooks (one fixed and two hanging from the tail). If the fishing is slow, head for one of the eddies.

72 | **Dress up warm for ice-fishing at Devil's Lake**

76 | **A magnificent muskie comes to the hand of a happy angler**

75
Catch huge carp on the fly
Beaver Island, Lake Michigan
May to July
Carp

The US has a difficult relationship with carp and many anglers dismiss them as "trash fish," not worth a cast; here on Beaver Island and in the surrounding archipelago, however, things are different. About as far away from typical carp-fishing (multiple rods, bite alarms, bivvy tents, all night sessions) as it's possible to get, here carp are stalked by sight in the clear waters of the flats around the island and caught on flies. And catching a large carp—think 30 lb (13 kg) plus—on a fly-rod makes for an unforgettable experience.

76
Home of the mighty muskie
Lake St. Clair, Detroit, Michigan
June to December
Muskellunge, yellow perch, smallmouth bass

Detroit—"motor city" and home of Motown—while not closely associated with fishing, sits on the banks of Lake St. Clair—the little lake that didn't quite make it when they were choosing which waters to include in the Great Lakes complex. The fishery has more or less recovered from an outbreak of viral hemorrhagic septicemia in the early 2000s and the muskellunge population has developed a stronger genetic strain. That, combined with an increase in shoals of native shad, means that it is home to some mighty "muskies" indeed.

A black bass . . . just about the most intriguing, gutsy fish that swims

77
BUCKET LIST FISH: Black bass
LAKE AGUAMILPA, MEXICO

There are many freshwater bass species but the two big ones are the North American largemouth bass and its cousin the smallmouth. What fantastic fish they are. You can pursue them with bait, fly, or lure. They take poppers with gusto, and fight ten times over their weight—rarely more than 6 lb (2.7 kg) or so, 10 lb (4.5 kg) being about the maximum. There are anglers who would never fish for anything else. Now that the species has been introduced around the world, notably to Spain and France, there are many Europeans equally, and rightly, obsessed.

78
Bonito bossa nova, baby

Acapulco, Guerrero, Mexico
Winter to spring
Marlin, tuna, bonito

For some, Acapulco will always be associated with the Elvis Presley movie *Fun in Acapulco*. This is ironic given that Presley was barred from traveling to Mexico, so a double was used for the location shots. There's no such sleight of hand with the fishing charters, and although catches have gone off a little in recent years, an experienced captain will put you onto the fish. A freshly caught bonito, glistening like a jewel, is a sight to see.

79
Big fish near the beach

Barra De Navidad, Costalegre, Jalisco, Mexico
November to March for tuna, June to August for marlin
Marlin, tuna

With its sandy beaches and small-town atmosphere, it's tempting to cast Barra De Navidad (which translates as "Christmas Sandbar") as a beach-vacation destination. However, monsters dwell offshore, and there are plenty of charters to take anglers out to find marlin and huge tuna (100 lb; 45 kg). On the way, expect to see whales, dolphins, and sea turtles. It's magical.

80
Bass of a lifetime

Lake El Salto, Mazatlán, Sinaloa, Mexico
April to June
Largemouth bass

This artificial lake is a magnet for wildlife, and anglers who stop to look up are likely to see black bears, pumas, wolves, coyotes, and white-tailed deer; look even higher up for peregrine falcons, black eagles, kestrels, osprey, and Harris hawks. The huge population of bass originally came from Florida and have flourished in El Salto's warm waters; while the average size is 5 to 6 lb (2.3 to 2.7 kg), the lake record is over 18 lb (8.2 kg).

81
All year trophy fishing

Lake Baccarac, Sinaloa, Mexico
All year
Largemouth bass

Many visitors to this lake in the Sierra Madre mountain range average forty to eighty fish a day, with at least a handful weighing almost 10 lb (4.5 kg). The lake's shad population ensures the table is never bare for the bass with their fabulously hinged jaws. Often the only thing that gets in the way of hooking a truly big one is all the "little" 4 lb (1.8 kg) guys that'll grab the lure first.

82
In the footsteps of privateers
Mazatlán, Sinaloa, Mexico
May to November
Sailfish, marlin

Famous among English and Spanish sailors in the 1600s, the port of Mazatlán is one of the finest natural harbors in the world—it offered shelter from any storms and was deep enough for the galleons of the time. Sir Thomas Cavendish, an infamous privateer, hid there and re-supplied while waiting for the *Santa Ana* to lumber past, its hold stuffed with hundreds of thousands of Spanish pesos; there was so much that Cavendish couldn't steal it all. These days, the harbor is a base for sport-anglers who hunt a different prey—marlin and sailfish.

83
The world's richest fishing grounds
Los Cabos, Baja, Mexico
July to October
Blue marlin, black marlin

Home to the famous Arch of Cabo San Lucas—carved from limestone by the wind and the water—and a favorite of vacationing celebrities, Los Cabos, at the tip of the 1,000 mi (1,609 km) long Baja Peninsula, remains one of the richest marlin fisheries anywhere in the world. Indeed, Cabos hosts the annual Bisbee's Black and Blue Marlin Tournament which, at the time of writing, has a jackpot that averages $3.5 million.

82 | **Hooked up to a marlin near the port of Mazatlán**

83 | **The sight Los Cabos' marlin anglers yearn to see**

The peerless permit is possibly the top target for fly fishers worldwide

84
BUCKET LIST FISH: Permit
ISLA BLANCA, MEXICO

This magnificent fish of warm seas can be found all over the world—as far as Oman, but perhaps at its best in Belize, Florida, and the Mexican Yucatán Peninsula. It inhabits deeper water and loves wrecks, but many would agree that the ultimate permit catches are taken from the flats, and preferably on the fly. Wading, even carefully, can alert these wary fish, so a skiff or a kayak can offer the best approach. An 8 wt rod, 10–12 lb (4.5–5.4 kg) leader, a crab-fly pattern, and plenty of backing and you are in business. Fancy a real challenge? Why not attempt the famed Inshore Grand Slam . . . a snook, tarpon, bonefish, and permit in the same day.

SOUTH AND CENTRAL AMERICA

GALAPAGOS ISLANDS

FALKLAND ISLANDS

SOUTH AND CENTRAL AMERICA: ENTRY LIST

85   Permit Alley, Belize
86   Tarpon Caye, Belize
87   The Drop, Belize Barrier Reef,
       Belize
88   Turneffe Atoll, Belize
89   Isla Mujeres, Yucatan Peninsula
90   Port San José, Guatemala
91   Port San José, Guatemala
92   Port San José, Guatemala
93   Pacific Coast, Nicaragua
94   Indio Maiz rain forest, Nicaragua
95   El Castillo, San Juan River,
       Nicaragua
96   San Juan del Sur, Nicaragua
97   San Juan del Sur, Nicaragua
98   Pacific Coast, Nicaragua
99   Rio San Juan, Nicaragua
100 Tortuguero, Limón, Costa Rica
101 Rio Colorado, Costa Rica
102 Barra del Colorado coast,
       Limón Province, Costa Rica
103 Barra del Colorado coast,
       Limón Province, Costa Rica
104 Tortuguero, Limón Province,
       Costa Rica
105 Guanacaste, Costa Rica
106 Lake Arenal, Costa Rica
107 Los Sueños, Puntarenas Province,
       Costa Rica
108 Osa Peninsula, Costa Rica
109 Quepos, Costa Rica
110 Savegre River, Puntarenas
       Province, Costa Rica
111 Tamarindo, Costa Rica
112 Tuna Coast, Panama
113 Panama
114 Gatun Lake, Panama
115 Acklins Island, Bahamas
116 Bight of Acklins, Acklins Island,
       Bahamas
117 Andros, Bahamas
118 Andros Barrier Reef, Bahamas
119 Crooked Island, Bahamas
120 Bimini, Bahamas
121 Freeport, Grand Bahama, Bahamas

122 Bahamas
123 Cayo Largo, Cuba
124 Isla de la Juventud, Cuba
125 Jardines de la Reina, Cuba
126 Lake Redonda, Cuba
127 Varadero, north of Hicacos
       Peninsula, Cuba
128 Turks and Caicos
129 Guadeloupe
130 Guadeloupe
131 Island of Iguanas, Martinique
132 Island of Iguanas, Martinique
133 Port of Spain, Trinidad and Tobago
134 Bahia Solano, Pacific Coast,
       Colombia
135 Vichada River, Colombia
136 Tomo River, Orinoco River Basin,
       Colombia
137 Tomo River, El Tuparro National
       Natural Park, Colombia
138 El Placer Ridge, La Guaira,
       Venezuela
139 Los Roques, Venezuela
140 Orinoco Delta, Venezuela
141 Los Roques, Venezuela
142 Cabedelo, Brazil
143 Mamiraua Reserve, Manaus, Brazil
144 Pantanal, Brazil
145 Upper River Negro, Brazil
146 River Negro, Brazil
147 Sierra de Bocaina National Park,
       Rio de Janeiro/São Paulo, Brazil
148 Camaiú River tributary rapids,
       Amazonas, Brazil
149 Camaiú River, Amazonas, Brazil
150 Autazes, Amazon Basin, Brazil
151 Amazon Basin, Brazil
152 The Mamiraua Reserve, Brazil
153 Flooded forests, Madeira System,
       Amazonas, Brazil
154 Urubu River, Amazonas, Brazil
155 Madeira River, Amazonas, Brazil
156 Madeira River System, Amazonas,
       Brazil

157 Sucundurí River still water,
       Amazonas, Brazil
158 Acarí River backwaters,
       Amazonas, Brazil
159 Acarí River still water,
       Amazonas, Brazil
160 Sorubí River, Amazonas, Brazil
161 Sucundurí River fast water,
       Amazonas, Brazil
162 Sucundurí River "lakes,"
       Amazonas, Brazil
163 Canumã River, Amazonas, Brazil
164 Sucundurí River deep pools,
       Amazonas, Brazil
165 Warrah, Chartres, and Murrell
       Rivers, San Carlos, Falkland
       Islands
166 Malleo River, Patagonia, Argentina
167 Uruguay River, Uruguay
168 Salto Grande Dam, La Zona,
       Uruguay River, Uruguay/
       Argentina
169 Rio Grande, Tierra del Fuego,
       Argentina
170 Chrome River, Los Lagos, Chile
171 Puelo River, Los Lagos, Chile
172 Agua Negra and Sécure Rivers,
       Tsimané, Bolivia
173 Casaré and Panchene,
       Santa Cruz, Bolivia
174 Araza River, Peru
175 Iquitos, Amazon Basin, Peru
176 Punta Sal, Tumbes, Peru
177 Sacred Valley Of The Incas,
       Cusco, Peru
178 Valley of Cañete, Peru
179 Galapagos Islands, Ecuador
180 Highlands of Ecuador, El Cajas
       National Park, Cuenca, Ecuador
181 Oriente (Amazon) Jungle,
       Cuyabeno Wildlife Reserve,
       Ecuador

86 | **Tarpon Caye is home to tarpon, the acrobat of the seas**

85

Fly-fish for wily permit in Permit Alley

Permit Alley, Belize

All year

Permit

Thirty miles (48 km) of shallow flats make this the perfect place to catch permit. You can find them here pretty much any time of year, though June is often thought of as the peak month. They hunt for crabs, shrimp, and shellfish in the coral, sand, and grasses, but like Permit Alley because the safety of deeper water isn't far away. Fly-fish for them in waist-deep or shallower water, and prepare to catch some keepers.

86

Hook mammoth-sized tarpon in Tarpon Caye

Tarpon Caye, Belize

April to September

Tarpon

Belize boasts great tarpon fishing year-round, but between April and September the big fish come, some of them upward of 200 lb (91 kg). These bottom feeders will bite on bait, crabs, clams, and flies, which makes fly-fishing for them particularly exciting. Find them in flats (where they're often visible in the water) and in the mangroves in river mouths. Be sure to bring the right rod for the weight of the fish you plan to land, or else you'll risk breaking the rod when you hook a big one.

87 | **A sailfish soars for the skies off Belize**

88 | **The glistening sheen of bonefish lights up the seas**

87
Troll for a world record
The Drop, Belize Barrier Reef, Belize
March to May
Marlin, sailfish

Enormous marlin have been caught in Belize, so with luck you could just be the next world-record holder. Though the season is year-round, the peak is in late spring, early summer. You'll want to head to the far side of the Barrier Reef to a spot anglers call The Drop. Because of this area's plunging depths, the marlin and sailfish fishing is second to none here.

88
Chase the "golden" bonefish
Turneffe Atoll, Belize
All year
Bonefish

Great bonefish can be found in many places, but few can boast of catching the elusive "golden," which are often larger than other fish in the school and frequently swim in the center. Catch one and you'll know instantly why they call them golden; they're a bright, beautiful yellow-green. Precise casting is key to getting the lure in the right place, but the numbers are in your favor. Year-round bonefish fishing is possible here, and anglers rave about catching 6 to 10 lb (2.7 to 4.5 kg) specimens.

89
BUCKET LIST
FISH: Sailfish
ISLA MUJERES, YUCATAN
PENINSULA

Sailfish swims in both the
Atlantic and Pacific Oceans,
but the Pacific fish grows
virtually twice the size. Both
varieties are great trophies,
perhaps the most beautiful
and exotically colored of all
game fish. When coming to
the bait or fly, the sailfish
colors-up with excitement
and when hooked glows with
colors of deep, dark blue on
the back and silver below.
The bars along the flank
turn lavender as the fastest
fish in the ocean makes the
reel sing. Fly-fishing is the
peak of achievements, but
play the fish hard to avoid a
shark attack and to facilitate
a successful release.

**Nature's masterpiece—the
coloration of a sailfish fin is
unmissable and unforgettable.**

90
Thrill and challenge in Guatemala's warm waters
Port San José, Guatemala
All year, best in September and October
Blue marlin

Most anglers head to the Pacific waters off the coast of Guatemala for sailfish, although the region also abounds with marlin, including blues, blacks, and stripes. Most of the action takes place in the waters off the fishing town of San José in an area known as The Pocket: a vast underwater canyon that abounds with baitfish, thereby attracting scores of game fish. Averaging 300 to 600 lb (136 to 272 kg), blue marlin can be caught year-round, although early fall is usually the best time.

91
Catch and release in the world's sailfishing hotspot
Port San José, Guatemala
November to June
Pacific sailfish

The waters off the coast of Guatemala offer some of the best sailfishing opportunities in the world, with sailfish reaching on average 80 to 120 lb (36 to 54 kg). Currents moving east from Mexico and west from Panama meet in the calm waters of the Pacific coast, creating nutrient-rich waters that attract scores of baitfish and game fish. Guatemala has strict conservation laws to protect sailfish, so all billfishing is catch-and-release with bait rigged with circle hooks.

90 | **A Guatemalan marlin cleaves the waves off Port San José**

92
Net one of the world's fastest fish

Port San José, Guatemala
September and October
Striped marlin

As well as being home to mind-boggling numbers of aggressive sailfish, the waters off the coast of Guatemala host three varieties of marlin species. One of the fastest fish in the world, the striped marlin is less common than blue marlin, although you still stand a good chance of landing one (or more). You'll be in for the fight of your life as it skips and leaps through the air and across the surface in an acrobatic dance.

93
Beautiful dorado congregate off the coast

Pacific Coast, Nicaragua
All year
Dorado

The brilliant-colored dorado is one of the prettiest saltwater fish, as well as being one of the tastiest. The shelf that runs the length of the continent has currents that favor this and other large species, but much closer to shore, currents and channels bring these beauties in. Charter with a local who knows the area and you may only have to go 5 mi (8 km) offshore to catch all the dorado you want, as well as others, like roosterfish or wahoo.

92| **In the crystal ocean of Guatemala, a marlin rounds up its prey**

Fishing dreams in the rain forests of the Indio Maiz

94
Pristine and protected rain forest
Indio Maiz rain forest, Nicaragua
All year
Tarpon, tiger bass, rainbow bass

It's not just the fishing here, it's the chance to be fishing in a jungle so immaculate it's like something out of a movie set. Miles upon miles of virgin, untouched forest, with a river that holds all the fish of your dreams. Giant tarpon, gorgeous rainbow bass, and tiger bass are easily caught, and while you wait for that tug on the line, you may catch keel-billed toucans passing overhead or spot glittering poison dart frogs clinging to the branches. It's wilderness fishing at its absolute best.

The colorful keel-billed toucan

A strawberry poison-dart frog

Wild sport with a tarpon

95

Fortress fishing

El Castillo, San Juan River, Nicaragua
All year, but best March to September
Atlantic tarpon, bull shark, machaca,
gafftopsail catfish

The San Juan River runs from Lake Nicaragua
into the Caribbean. It runs through tropical
jungle with wildlife and flora. The water system
is one of the only places in the world where you
can catch sharks in freshwater, the bull shark. A
serious number of tarpon reside both in the lake
and, especially, in the river. The picturesque
village of El Castillo, named for the seventeenth-
century Spanish fortress there, is partly built on
posts in the river; and the only way to get there
is by boat. There are so many tarpon that the
locals catch them by spear fishing. Anglers can
catch tarpon and bull sharks undisturbed, and
there are others to catch on light tackle such as
machaca, cichlids, and gafftopsail catfish.

96

Hunt for mammoth marlin off San Juan del Sur

San Juan del Sur, Nicaragua
December to January
Blue, black, striped marlin

It could be hard to find better marlin
fishing than the winter months in San
Juan del Sur. This quiet fishing town is in
a sheltered bay, and just offshore is where
the action happens. Look for the "blue
water," keep fingers crossed and you may
see fish weighing 800 lbs (360 kg) or
more, and if you're lucky, you might just
hook one. They are highly migratory,
but striped, blue, and black marlin all
congregate here, so your chances are as
good as they'll get.

**95 | Bull shark, tarpon, gafftopsail catfish . . .
you'll catch them all in the San Juan River**

97
Find hard-fighting sailfish near the shore
San Juan del Sur, Nicaragua
November to May
Sailfish

Peaceful, sheltered San Juan del Sur is a fishing charter mecca, and offers excellent sailfishing much of the year, with the best fishing in May to November. These beautiful fish are fantastic fighters and aren't far offshore—landing one takes cunning and skill. You can be sure that a few fish will be the ones that got away. The ones that don't will dazzle. Catch and release is favored here, but other smaller species may become your tasty dinner.

97 | **San Juan is beloved by sailfish aficionados**

98
Find wahoo as tall as you are
Pacific Coast, Nicaragua
May to September
Wahoo

There's no doubt about it, wahoo is a wonderful sport fish. Fast, sleek, beautiful, and good fighters, they make a day on the water worth it every time. Swimming at speeds up to 60 mph (100 kmh), they are also one of the ocean's fastest fish, making catching them all the more of a thrill. The best part about fishing this section of Nicaragua is that you'll likely have the sea all to yourself. It's still relatively unknown to tourists, and unfished.

98 | **A silver and iridescent blue wahoo**

99 | **An impressive red snapper**

99
Placid waters and great stock

Rio San Juan, Nicaragua
All year
Jungle tarpon, rainbow bass, snooks, snapper

Most commercial sportfishing stopped for decades due
to the Nicaraguan political turmoil, which allowed the
tarpon, rainbow bass, and snook populations to recover
and grow. Today's Rio San Juan offers excellent fishing,
and conservation is well-regulated, so big fish aren't being
depleted at rates they are elsewhere. Consequently you
can expect a thrilling day on the water, with tarpon
sometimes weighing above 200 lb (90 kg). Snook,
snapper, and rainbow bass are other prize fish you're
liable to land.

100
Wildlife and great sportfishing

Tortuguero, Limón, Costa Rica
All year
Cichlids, machaca

If you need a break from the open ocean and want to give
something else a try, consider the clear, placid waters of
Tortuguero ("the turtle hunter"). Charters run on the
famous canal, but you can get farther off the grid by
venturing down some of the area's many rivers. Vegetarian
machaca and a number of cichlids are the primary catch,
but expect snook, tarpon, and rainbow bass to be possible
as well. The wildlife out of the water is impressive too, with
excellent birding and animal spotting.

100 | **You never know what you'll catch in the waters of Tortuguero**

A Costa Rican tarpon jumps so close you can feel the spray on your face and the taste of salt on your tongue

101
BUCKET LIST FISH: Tarpon
RIO COLORADO, COSTA RICA

Is there a harder, more acrobatic fighting-fish in the waters of the world than the tarpon? Probably not, and that is why tarpon is pursued obsessively in the inshore waters and lagoons of the western Atlantic, the Caribbean, the west coast of Central America, and the coast of northwest Africa.

These silver-scaled giants can reach 200 lb (90 kg) and more, and fishing for them by lure or fly is always an electric experience. They come so close, in such shallow water, that the experience is eyeball to eyeball; a white-knuckle angling adventure.

102
Fish with the seasons off the lush Barra del Colorado coast
Barra del Colorado coast, Limón, Costa Rica
May to October
Jack crevalle, Atlantic tarpon, tripletail

The fish here vary with the seasons, but what doesn't change is the incredible catches just a few hundred yards offshore. Look for jack crevalle in channels, on reefs, and sometimes in river mouths if the water permits good casting. Tripletail, some of them behemoths, are usually found January to June. Tarpon is another easy one to catch. If you're fishing river mouths, be wary of crocodiles, but the real catch may be getting there, as this lush, delightful spot is as remote as Costa Rica gets. Plan on some creative chartering when you make reservations.

103
Tarpon city
Barra del Colorado, Limón Province, Costa Rica
March to May and September to December for tarpon, all year for other species
Atlantic tarpon, jack crevalle, tripletail, sharks

As well as being part of a nature refuge, the Caribbean coast at the Rio Colorado estuary is a world-class tarpon fishery, with many big fishing-lodges and commercial fishing. The locals concentrate on catching sharks and spiny lobsters, leaving anglers to enjoy species like the tarpon, jack, tripletail, and other fighting fish. The standard way to catch these fish here is with big, hairy jigs. The jig-hook needs to be extremely sharp to set in the bony mouth of the tarpon; the other species are just as happy with the jigs, and much easier to hook.

102 | **Superb jack crevalle in clear Costa Rican waters**

103 | **The Caribbean coast offers great tarpon fishing**

Electrifying convict cichlid

The sight of nesting green turtles enhances any trip

The jungle biodiversity of Tortuguero has a lushness mirrored only in the richness of the fishing

104

Jungle paradise

Tortuguero, Limón Province, Costa Rica

All year

Tropical gar, common snook, cichlids, machaca

Tortuguero is situated on the Caribbean coast, and is globally recognized for its national park, bird-life, nesting sea turtles, and poison arrow frogs. The jungle biodiversity here is only rivaled by the Amazon. Also, the fishing is exciting, with everything from hammerhead sharks and tarpon, to colorful cichlids. Even large tarpon venture in the narrow jungle canals, but with light tackle there is a world of special, exotic fish species to catch: cichlids in many colors and sizes, aggressive machaca, snook, and even the tropical gar which can reach a length of over 4 ft (125 cm).

105 | What a comb on this rooster!

106 | Lake Arenal is a popper fisher's paradise

105
Fly-fish for quirky roosterfish
Guanacaste, Costa Rica
All year
Roosterfish

Year-round fishing for roosterfish makes Guanacaste a perfect spot for anglers wanting to add this unique, quirky fighter to their bucket list. With its beautiful "cockerel's comb" dorsal fin and its stunning patterned scales, it's really a fish to behold. Fly-fish for smaller ones or take a boat out offshore for larger fish. The truly lucky anglers won't just get a roosterfish, but a sailfish too . . . and even see some humpback whales. Plenty of pockets of pristine coastline make it a beautiful spot for a beach vacation, too.

106
Coax mammoth-sized rainbow bass from their watery lairs
Lake Arenal, Costa Rica
January to May
Rainbow bass

Nicknamed "handsome one" in Spanish, the *guapote*, or rainbow bass, of Lake Arenal is second to none, especially in the dry season when lake levels drop and these monsters have shallower places to hide. These cichlids (not true bass at all) are stunning and the world record weight is 15 lb (6.8 kg). Most of the ones you'll catch are smaller, but you never know what's lurking there. Fish for them with poppers, and find roots and submerged trees, their favorite hiding spots. If the lake waters are glassy, the near-perfect Arenal Volcano nearby can seem almost close enough to touch.

107
A competition for behemoths
Los Sueños, Puntarenas Province, Costa Rica
December to June
Blue marlin

This upscale coastal resort is only an hour's drive from Costa Rica's capital, San José, and features luxury accommodation, several championship-level golf courses, rain forest hiking, water sports, and inshore and offshore deep sea fishing, all in the verdant setting of Costa Rica's "Green Coast." It's also home to the Los Sueños Signature Triple Crown tournament which brings together anglers from all over the world to fish three legs every January, February, and March in search of the gargantuan sailfish, spearfish, and marlin that swim in these waters.

108
Catch dorado in azure waters
Osa Peninsula, Costa Rica
December to January
Dorado

Dorado are here year-round but at their peak in the winter months when ocean currents bring these gorgeous trophy-fish in large numbers. It's not uncommon to hook fish as tall as you are. And with so much of the peninsula protected by the breathtaking Corcovado National Park, you're sure to have an easier time convincing family members that this spot will be somewhere everyone will enjoy.

107 | The coast is a magnet for marlin and sailfish

108 | Dorado are one of the most beguiling species

109
Find fabulous sailfish in the deep waters off Quepos
Quepos, Costa Rica
November to April
Sailfish

Costa Rica boasts year-round fin-fishing, and the sailfish is no exception, however the months of November to April are truly something else. You don't have to go too far offshore to find them. Sometimes it's only an hour or so before you've reached the tell-tale bird activity that indicates sailfish are below. In many parts of the world, you're lucky to even spot a sailfish, let alone to catch one. Here, they're often seen multiple times in one boat ride.

110
Fly-fish for machaca, snook, and snapper in a pristine river
Savegre River, Puntarenas Province, Costa Rica
All year
Machaca, snook, snapper

If you're planning to fish in the waters of the upper Savegre River remember to pack flies tied to resemble flowers and leaves. That's because these will entice the elusive machaca, a vegetarian relative of the piranha, giving some anglers their catch of a lifetime. This river is also known to harbor snook and snapper, so a charter here, often in small craft and floating with the current, has something for everyone.

109 | **Look out for an extraordinary number of fish off the coast of Costa Rica**

112 | **A 150-lb (68-kg) yellowfin tuna is brought to the surface by a fisherman**

111
See all three types of marlin on one trip

Tamarindo, Costa Rica
June to December
Marlin, sailfish

Known for its great surfing beaches, tiny, off-the-map Tamarindo has sportfishing opportunities that shouldn't be overlooked. You don't have to go far offshore to find all three types of marlin—blue, black, and striped—as well as its billfish cousin, the sailfish. The continental shelf drops off just a half-hour from the shoreline, meaning deepwater fishing is practically a stone's throw away. Excellent inshore fishing opportunities, too, mean this spot deserves a place on your bucket list.

112
They don't call it the "Tuna Coast" for nothing

Tuna Coast, Panama
January to May
Yellowfin tuna

The Tuna Coast, on the Pacific side of Panama, may be the yellowfin tuna capital of the world, with incredible fishing from January to May, but it can last until August. Bait balls rise to the surface and when there's a feeding frenzy you can count on catching fish with almost every cast. Though the yellowfin record was caught off of Cabo San Lucas, this region gets the same biggies year after year, so the next record may be set by you. You never know.

113 | A sailfish on fly is the ultimate achievement

114 | A peacock in its coat of many colors

113
Where there are sailfish and marlin pretty much anywhere
Panama
May to September
Marlin, Pacific sailfish

They may call it the Tuna Coast but that doesn't mean all you'll catch is tuna, especially if you come for the warmer months of May through September. That's when Pacific sailfish and marlin are plentiful, some coming close enough to be caught right from shore with a lucky cast. Most anglers head out for deeper water, but you don't have to go too far offshore to start getting lucky. Either way, it's a great time to be in Panama and you're sure to catch some amazing fish.

114
Peacock paradise
Gatun Lake, Panama
All year
Peacock Bass

There are bigger "peacocks" in the world, but Gatun Lake holds huge numbers of them and is a special location in itself. The lake was built a century ago by submerging an area of rain forest, and now feeds the Panama Canal with freshwater. It is huge—160 square mi (415 square km)—and an important conservation area. Fishing boats are easily available, and angling is done by lure, bait, and fly for fish averaging 2 to 5 lb (1 to 2 kg). December to May is the dry season so fish close to the bank structure. May to December is the wet season and fishing happens farther out in open water.

115
A bonefisher's treasure island
Acklins Island, Bahamas
All year, but best from March to April
Bonefish

Acklins is positioned at the far south of the Bahamas and is
best accessed by light plane. Its relative remoteness has for
years ensured this is a peaceful place and so it has escaped
some of the fanfare surrounding better known "bone"
destinations. That's not to say you'll find unfished water
here, but the extensive flats are quiet and there are very big
bonefish to be found. There are excellent guides available
too, and they tend to be local people who have known the
Acklins' waters since childhood. This is the essence of the
experience. Great fishing in a natural, unspoiled, and
genuinely welcoming place.

115 | **The bountiful seas of the
Bahamas offer the best bonefishing**

116
Fly-fish for barracuda in a vast, shallow lagoon

Bight of Acklins, Acklins Island, Bahamas

All year

Barracuda

Fly-fishing in the Bight of Acklins is a once-in-a-lifetime experience: a vast, shallow lagoon surrounded by gorgeous islands on three sides. You can cast from shore or use a boat, experienced anglers look to the fly-rod. Barracuda are ever-hungry predators who will strike on live bait or needlefish lures, and chumming the water helps to lure them. In quieter moments, take the time to enjoy the incredible colors of the lagoon and the gentle green of the island.

117
The bonefish El Dorado

Andros, Bahamas

All year

Bonefish, permit

This truly is one of the world's great bonefish destinations. Vast shoals of the species live in the wide variety of water available and the average size of "bones" is on the high side, between 4 and 6 lb (1.8 and 2.7 kg), although trophies of double-figures are often sighted and there to be caught. Many would say that the Middle and South Bights give the best of the fishing but there are thousands of acres of prime fishing-grounds here. Great lodges, great local guides, and the permit arrive between April and July to give added spice.

118

Fish off one of the world's longest barrier reefs

Andros Barrier Reef, Bahamas

June to August

Amberjack, grouper, triggerfish

Few places in the world can boast of deepwater fishing close to shore, but Andros Barrier Reef in the Bahamas is one. The sixth-longest reef in the world is near the shore, but just beyond it, waters drop to over 2,000 ft (610 m). In places, it is close to 1 mi (1,600 m) deep. The depth, currents, and temperatures make the fishing here incredible all year, but in the summer months the amberjack, grouper, and triggerfish are at their peak. As well as the deep water, there are numerous shore and shallow lagoon spots to fly-fish or cast from, too.

119

Blue water heaven

Crooked Island, Bahamas

October to March for wahoo, April to September for tuna and dolphin

Wahoo, tuna, dolphinfish

Crooked Island is surrounded by a barrier reef and that, along with the island's remoteness, has kept commercial fishing at bay. The result: almost every blue-water species can be caught here, but tuna, wahoo, and dolphinfish are the three stars of the island. There is deep water close to shore, so long boat trips are not necessary. Most sport is had by trolling, but the experienced fly-angler can have great sport, especially with the strong runs of tuna. A skipper will often attract a school of fish by chumming and then fly-action is a real option.

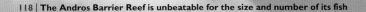

118 | **The Andros Barrier Reef is unbeatable for the size and number of its fish**

120
Catch bonefish in pristine estuaries and lagoons
Bimini, Bahamas
September, January to March
Bonefish

Bonefish are easily spooked but are in such numbers here in Bimini that anglers can expect a quick strike with a well-placed cast. Bonefish put up a fantastic fight, and while they are usually in the 3 to 4 lb (1.4 to 1.8 kg) range here, they're often larger. Record fish have topped 15 lb (6.8 kg), and anglers will swear there are 20 lb (9 kg) monsters lurking as well. Precision casting is key, as they love to hide in mangrove roots.

121
Channel your inner Hemingway
Freeport, Grand Bahama, Bahamas
April to August, best in June and July
Blue marlin

Blue marlin here can reach upwards of 1,000 lb (454 kg) and they average in the mid-200s (around 115 kg). This incredible fighter can challenge even the most experienced angler so prepare for a workout as you reel in one of the world's most famous and sought-after fish. When they're hungry, marlin are known to hit lures multiple times, so don't give up if you can't hook them right away. If you've got a competitive streak, come during one of the Bahamas billfish championships and you may walk away with the prize.

121 | **The marlin sport off Freeport offers serious numbers of colossal fish**

Pound for pound, the fastest fish in the ocean

122
BUCKET LIST FISH: Bonefish
BAHAMAS

Although it might never even grow to 20 lb (9 kg), bonefish are still the fly fishers' marine target of the century. You'd never believe a 5 lb (2.3 kg) fish could strip such huge lengths of line off a reel until you have experienced the first, smoking run of a bonefish. "Bones" are found worldwide in tropical coastal waters and they are pursued on the flats where they feed on shrimp and crabs and can be stalked and sight-fished. Typically, you are wading or fishing from a skiff, watching for muddied water and tails of feeding fish. Put out a crab-fly imitation, twitch it back, and wait for fireworks.

123
Go for a grand slam
Cayo Largo, Cuba
November to June
Bonefish, permit, tarpon

If the idea of landing a 100 lb (45 kg) tarpon or catching a Super Grand Slam (snook, tarpon, bonefish, permit) sounds appealing, then consider making your next charter in Cuba's azure Cayo Largo ("Long Key"). Catching tarpon in the 40 lb (18 kg) range is common, but migratory megafish come through as well, meaning that your day may get very exciting fast. Even if not much happens fishing-wise, though, it's a spectacular spot, with shallow waters and pristine beaches that are thus far still off many tourists' maps.

124
Hunt bonefish and permit on the hard flats of Isla de la Juventud
Isla de la Juventud, Cuba
November to July
Bonefish, permit, tarpon

Tarpon, bonefish, and permit, aka a Grand Slam, all can be caught in the shallow flats of Cuba's Isla de la Juventud, the "Isle of Youth." The network of deeper channels offers plenty of spots for the biggies to hide, with the shallower areas chock full of excellent smaller fish. Come during the early winter to catch this prime fishing spot at its peak.

124 | Glowing sunset on the famed Island Of Youth

125

Fish for bonefish and permit in these spectacular "gardens"

Jardines de la Reina, Cuba

All year

Bonefish, permit

If you like the idea of looking to the horizon and not seeing another boat, Cuba's Jardines de la Reina ("Queen's Gardens") may be perfect for you. Located 70 mi (110 km) offshore, these "gardens" are a series of keys, shoals, and flats that attract bonefish and permit all year, as well as plenty of other species. Even better, these waters are protected against commercial fishing and thus there's all the more waiting for you and your favorite lure.

126

Hook largemouth bass the size of watermelons

Lake Redonda, Cuba

All year

Largemouth bass, trout

Some call Cuba the bass-fishing capital of the world, and if not, it's certainly a top contender. Catching anything less than 5 lb (2.25 kg) bass seems paltry, and Lake Redonda is one of the top spots in the island to find bass. Now part of an ambitious sustainable tourism initiative, the lake has some of the largest bass Cuba has to offer. Trout here are similarly gargantuan.

126 | Lake Redonda offers spectacular fishing

127 | Gray pelicans on the shore at Varadero

128 | Fish in the magical mangrove flats

127
Fly-fish or troll for marlin and other billfish
Varadero, north of Hicacos Peninsula, Cuba
November to March
Billfish, marlin

In the vast Atlantic triangle between Key West, the Bahamas, and Cuba lies spectacular billfishing, and Varadero offers easy access, as well as everything else beautiful Cuba has to offer. Catch them with flies or by trolling, and prepare for a great, challenging fight—these incredible fish are known to use every trick in the book to escape your line.

128
Find elusive fish in the mangrove flats
Turks and Caicos
November to July
Bonefish

Wily and evasive bonefish congregate in the mangrove channels here in the Turks and Caicos, giving anglers who fly-fish excellent opportunity to hook one . . . or several. You can wade out or fish from a skiff—either way, the chances are fantastic. The entire archipelago is tailor-made for bonefish, with shallow flats and enticing channels that lend themselves for perfect fishing.

129 | Guadeloupe's flats are a stunning venue for the salt-fly angler

129
Where the bonefish thrive
Guadeloupe
All year
Bonefish

Guadeloupe's flats thrive with fish species, including bonefish, tarpon, snooks, and permits, who feast on small crustaceans and sea urchins. They can be targeted in shallow water when they're on the lookout for food, making the Caribbean's crystal-clear waters the perfect setting for saltwater fly-fishing. Use flies, lures, or bait—shrimp is a good choice. Full of stamina, bonefish will give you a strong fight.

130
Pedal kayak on the lookout for tarpon
Guadeloupe
October to May
Tarpon

Renowned for their acrobatic jumps and prized for their fight, tarpon are particularly stubborn fish that are among the most difficult to land. They are primarily found in coastal waters, estuaries, and mangroves, with Guadeloupe offering one of the best spots to catch them. You'll need a stealthy approach not to scare them away; pedal kayaking is a great choice, allowing you to fish discreetly. Spinning with lures (use streamers of different colors) and fly-fishing are the best techniques.

131
Fishing for the world's trophy fish
Island of Iguanas, Martinique
December to February
Blue marlin

Martinique's waters are renowned for big game fishing, with blue marlin—probably the anglers' most sought-after fish—commonly found hunting baitfish offshore. Catch them with dead bait such as bonito, skipjack tuna, or mullet, or troll the waters with artificial lures. An exciting catch, these trophy fish are most often found near the surface of the water where temperatures are warmer.

132
Trick dorado with artificial lures
Island of Iguanas, Martinique
February to June
Dorado

The island of Martinique forms the boundary of the Caribbean Sea and the Atlantic Ocean. Its offshore waters abound with dorado, or mahi-mahi, recognizable from their long dorsal fin, bluntly shaped head, and vibrant, shiny coloring. They are an aggressive fish that will bite virtually any lure and are renowned for putting up a strong fight, making them very popular with big game anglers. If using dead bait, you could go for mackerel, jack, or ballyhoo.

133
Troll for kingfish and Spanish mackerel
Port of Spain, Trinidad and Tobago
November to April
Kingfish, Spanish mackerel

If you like trolling for seemingly never-ending fish, then set your sights for Port of Spain, Trinidad and Tobago, where you can head out for a day of fishing and never need to cast. These beautiful fish will just keep hitting whatever you put out for them, and pulling them in couldn't be easier. Get three, five, ten in a day. Take them home or release, it's up to you.

134
Come any time of year for great saltwater fishing
Bahia Solano, Pacific Coast, Colombia
All year
Dorado, marlin, roosterfish, sailfish

What makes fishing good here is the fact that you can pick any month of the calendar and expect to have a great time with some impressive catches. The big draws are dorado, marlin, roosterfish, and sailfish; each are best caught in particular months, but there's always something exciting in these waters. Not surprisingly, there's fantastic snorkeling and scuba here as well.

135
Fight pugnacious peacocks
Vichada River, Colombia
January to April
Peacock bass

Rushing through the Matavén forest, the Rio Vichada abounds with giant peacock bass, with some specimens weighing more than 20 lb (9 kg). Enjoy some thrilling topwater action using surface poppers or work big flies as you look out for other predators including the powerful bicuda and mighty tambaqui, whose strike can be as violent as that of the peacock bass (they can easily snap off your reel and crush a saltwater hook).

136
Fish in the remote Tomo River
Tomo River, Orinoco River Basin, Colombia
January to March
Peacock bass, redtail catfish

Remote river campsites, hidden fishing holes, and incredible catches await anglers who head to Colombia's Tomo River. The prize fishes here are the massive peacock bass and gorgeous redtail catfish, both of which are frequently caught here. Stock conservation is foremost in mind, so all fishing is catch and release, ensuring these incredible biggies are still in the river for future fishing. This is true jungle fishing at its best, so plan for excitement . . . and bring that mosquito repellent.

135 | **The peacock bass of the Vichada River bristle with attitude**

137
Blazing beauty
Tomo River, El Tuparro National
Natural Park, Colombia
Mid-December to mid-March
Peacock bass

How extraordinary are peacock bass—these
beautiful fish of blazing colors! There are
eleven recognized sub-species now and
three, if not four, are caught in the Tomo,
including the mightiest of them all, the paca
acu bass. El Tuparro is one of Colombia's
most pristine ecosystems where hundreds of
mammal, bird, and fish species thrive and
butterflies swarm in clouds. Most anglers fish
with a fly here, large surface-poppers, or
streamers worked relatively fast. You are
asked to use single hooks for the safety
of the fish, but make them strong.

138
Watch some incredible white-marlin action
El Placer Ridge, La Guaira, Venezuela
August to December
White marlin

Lying about 12 mi (19 km) from the city of
La Guaira, La Guaira Bank is a plankton-rich
underwater ridge that bursts with nutrients
attracting tuna, wahoo, dorado, and white
marlin, making it one of the Caribbean's top
sportfishing destinations. Known in Spanish
as *El Placer* (pleasure), the bank is home to
one of the world's most impressive
concentrations of billfish, as well as huge
numbers of blue and white marlin. Mostly
taking place in the fall, its run of white
marlin is spectacular, with anglers easily
recording double-digit releases.

137 | **Experience heart-stopping sailfish action on the Tomo River**

139
Bonefish capital of the world

Los Roques, Venezuela
All year
Bonefish, permit, tarpon

Los Roques offers anglers an unparalleled number and variety of opportunities, most especially for "bones" on the almost endless flats. It was awarded national park status in 1972 and this has helped the area maintain its pristine beauty—it is said there are more pelicans than people here. Permit and tarpon also feature heavily in catches and it is far enough south that the worst of the hurricane season is avoided here.

140
Enjoy crystal-clear waters

Los Roques, Venezuela
January to May
Bonefish

Offering some of the Caribbean's best fly-fishing, the Los Roques archipelago comprises over 350 islands and cays, with a wealth of mangrove lagoons, flats, and coral banks. The crystal-clear waters abound with shoals of minnows, attracting game fish such as jacks, tarpon, and bonefish. You'll easily be able to target huge schools of bonefish as they take advantage of feeding opportunities. Keen fly fishers will be rewarded with opportunities for tailing fish, perfect for anglers who enjoy stalk-fishing on foot.

141
Tarpon fishing on the Orinoco Delta

Orinoco Delta, Venezuela
December to April
Tarpon

Located in eastern Venezuela, the fan-shaped Orinoco Delta is home to a myriad of distributaries, or *caños*, slowly running to the sea. The delta makes for one of the best fly-fishing tarpon-destinations, with large and aggressive tarpon requiring various fishing techniques—a knowledge of distance-casting is a plus. Floating lines are perfect to catch the tarpon on the flooded delta, although you may also want to consider fast-sinking lines to fish in deeper pools.

140 | Venezuelan bonefish are at their best at Los Roques

142
Test your strength in the open sea
Cabedelo, Brazil
October to May
Tuna, wahoo, sailfish, blue marlin

On the easternmost tip of South America, Cabedelo is only 25 mi (40 km) from where the continental shelf drops off, making this a great spot to fish for pelagic species. Head offshore to the temperate waters of the Atlantic to reel in huge fish including tuna, wahoo, and sailfish. You can test your strength as you battle with blue marlin—you won't easily forget the surface-display when one of them gets hooked.

143
Sustainable arapaima fishing
Mamiraua Reserve, Manaus, Brazil
August to December
Arapaima

At Mamiraua you'll be fishing in one of the largest protected rain forest areas in the world. All angling is done in partnership with the local people and the results protect 400 bird species, red river dolphins, black-faced squirrel monkeys, manatees, and an arapaima fishery that is beyond imagination. Fishing is centered on the Solimos river where fly-fishing for fish in excess of 300 lb (136 kg) is a reality. Use 12 wt gear and cast big surface-flies for fish you can see hunting.

142 | Shaped like a bullet, colored steel blue, Cabedelo wahoo are some of the quickest fish in the ocean

Fabulous big cats add spice to an expedition

A golden dorado breaks the surface

The Pantanal is a magnet for dorado fishers

144
Mind-boggling statistics
Pantanal, Brazil
March to June
Golden dorado

The Pantanal wetlands almost defy description. They cover more than 50,000 sq mi (129,500 sq km) and are home to 700 species of bird and a hundred types of mammal. For the angler, there are myriad rivers, lakes, and streams holding well over 200 fish species, including pacu, piranha, and the imperious golden dorado. It is the latter fish most anglers strive for and the Panatanal is a true fly fisher's paradise. Huge surface-feeding fish hit lures with ferocious abandon and the ensuing battle is as much out of the water as in it. The Taiamã Ecological Station is a wonderful base for this supreme angling adventure.

145

Fishing and conservation in harmony

Upper Rio Negro, Brazil

August to March, best from January to March

Peacock bass

The Rio Negro has to be one of the world's top peacock bass locations and it looks set to stay that way. Entry permits are now necessary to fish some of the best water. The money collected is used to protect local communities, forests, and the river. Anglers hire local guides, people who have ancient knowledge of the species and enrich the whole angling experience. And what an experience. Does any freshwater fish fight harder? Much of the fishing is done using big poppers which attract big fish, arguably the largest peacocks on the planet.

146

Fish the jet-black waters of the Rio Negro

Rio Negro, Brazil

September to January

Peacock bass

Head for the Rio Negro river basin in the heart of the Amazon rain forest and the peacock bass, or *tucunaré*, can reach about 20 lb; 9 kg. This prized freshwater fish forms a staple of Amazonian cuisine. Catch them by fly-fishing or spinning in shallow waters on one of the river's untouched tributaries or side channels—the fish will strike and a ferocious battle will ensue. The river's jet-black waters teem with marine species, including giant catfish and piranha.

145 | Peacock bass love the waters of the Upper Rio Negro

147

Wade for rainbow trout

Sierra de Bocaina National Park, Rio de
Janeiro/São Paulo, Brazil

May to early September

Rainbow trout

Lying across the states of Rio de Janeiro
and São Paulo, the protected rain forest of
Sierra de Bocaina National Park stretches
from the beaches of Paraty to the
mountainous hinterland. Trout was first
introduced to Brazil in 1949, and the
Mambucaba River, which crosses the
park, is one of the best places to fish for
it. It remains little-known to anglers—
for now. The best time is summer,
although mornings can be quite cold.
You'll need to wade in the river's chilly
waters, so a wading stick and warm gear
will come in handy.

147 | **The Mambucaba River holds rainbow trout**

148 | The common brycon is a star species in the tributaries of the Camaiú River

148
Amazon trout fishing
Camaiú River tributary rapids,
Amazonas, Brazil
July to October
Common brycon (South American trout)

Who would have thought that you
could go trout-fishing in the deep
jungle of the Amazon? Well, this is not
really a salmonid trout, but this fish
behaves and feels like the trout that
swims in colder climates. Small
tributary-streams of crystal-clear water
at little, rocky waterfalls in the Camaiú
River provide the fast water that this
predatory characin prefers. It takes
typical trout baits, such as small
spinners, small spoons, and wet flies,
and its fight is every bit as enjoyable
with jumps and powerful runs.

149
Electrifying fishing
Camaiú River, Amazonas, Brazil
August to October
Lowland electric eel

The Camaiú River is a gem in the Amazon. It is
rarely fished, and you can catch almost all the
interesting species in near record sizes. Electric
eels are hunters and scavengers. They will take
a piece of dead fish just as well as a live one. Their
electricity is not a laughing matter. They can easily
stun a large caiman, and they are considered
potentially lethal to people. They mainly stay far
in the river system where the water level doesn't
change as much. You find them exclusively in calm,
deep parts of the rivers and swamps, where they
lurk in ambush of prey. They can grow to 8 ft
(2.5 m) and weigh up to around 45 lb (20 kg),
but the average fish is between 4 and 20 lb (2 to
9 kg), and 3 to 6 ft (1 to 2 m) long.

150
Try for some of the world's largest freshwater species
Autazes, Amazon Basin, Brazil
June to December for pirarucú, June to March for piraiba catfish
Arapaima, piraiba catfish

The Juma River and Mamorí Lake regions in the municipal areas of Autazes are home to the arapaima, or *pirarucú*, one of the largest freshwater fish in the world, weighing a whopping 440 lb (200 kg), making this the perfect choice for anglers seeking to chase big fish. The piraiba, the largest catfish in the Amazon basin, is found in the deep river waters and undertakes long migrations to spawn. You'll need a powerful fishing-reel with large line-capacity—once hooked, you'll be in for a long battle before landing it.

151
Fish the slow-moving waters of Amazonian waterways
Amazon Basin, Brazil
June to December
Red oscar

Living in the warm, tropical waters of the Amazon River basin, the red oscar is an aggressive species that can be a challenge for anglers using fly-rods or light spinning tackle. Trolling, spin-casting, drift-fishing and bait-casting are all common fishing methods used to catch this dark-brown fish with red markings on its body. The fish have ocelli, or eyespots, on their tails, a defensive mechanism that confuses predators as to which end of the body is the head.

150 | **The peace is shattered by a hunting arapaima**

The magnificent arapaima are beautiful, rare, and one of the most desirable trophies in the angling world

152
BUCKET LIST FISH: Arapaima
THE MAMIRAUA RESERVE, BRAZIL

These extraordinary fish are beyond doubt the top prize from the Amazon catchment area. They are huge, 400 lb (180 kg) plus, beautiful, and rare. Arapaima periodically break the surface to take in air and this necessity makes them vulnerable to hunters who have exacted a terrible toll over the years. Yet arapaima are still there to be caught—and released of course—but make no mistake, this is one of the great remaining quests of the modern age. They have been successfully imported into Thailand where they can be caught in comfort from any one of several commercial waters.

153

Flooded forest predators

Flooded forests, Madeira System,
Amazonas, Brazil
September to November
Trahira (tigerfish)

The Amazon River system is prone to
enormous yearly changes in water level by as
much as 33 ft (10 m). That means the rain
forest is regularly flooded, and there are
lovely areas where you can walk among the
vegetation in crystal-clear water, and fish
between the trees; but keep an eye out for
the caimans. Many small fish take shelter
here, but there is one fish which specializes
in hunting in there, and that is the ferocious
trahira. The trahira is relatively small
compared to the other famous predators
such as peacock bass and arowana, but they
are so much fun to catch. The best baits are
colorful and noisy surface-lures, as well as
flies where possible.

153 | **The flooded forests of Amazonia**

154 | **A brycon will fight for your lure**

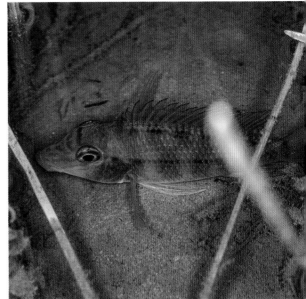

155 | **Eartheater cichlids are a fascinating target**

154
Work your lure under low-hanging Amazonian vegetation
Urubu River, Amazonas, Brazil
February to May
Brycon

Inhabiting the freshwater habitats of South America, the brycon, or *matrinchã*, is sometimes referred to as the South American trout, although it's not closely related to true trout. Fish with lures, poppers, and big flies under the trees (use fruit or spiders as bait), where you'll find the fish lurking beneath low-hanging vegetation; you may well spot them jumping out of the water to pluck seeds and fruits off the branches above. They're among the strongest fighting-fish in the Amazon and they will battle to get to your lure first.

155
Cichlid dreams
Madeira River, Amazonas, Brazil
All year, but best April to October
Various cichlids

Peacock bass are big cichlids, but there are many other fascinating cichlid species, of many shapes and colors, all over the Amazon. Some of the most dramatic are the pike cichlids, which, as the name suggests, are very much like pike in both shape and behavior. They are, however, much more colorful, as you would expect of tropical fish. Species like acaras, discus, and eartheater cichlids readily take small baits. They can be found mostly in shallow water, away from piranhas, and take small spinners, jigs, and flashy flies.

156
Unrivaled teeth
Madeira River System, Amazonas, Brazil
All year, when it is possible to enter the rivers
Piranhas

This is the largest tributary of the Amazon, contributing 15 percent of the water volume. Here, and all over the Amazon, there are large numbers of piranhas of various species. They are generally considered an annoyance, because they cut fishing lines with their razor-sharp teeth. However, they fight really well and they are good to eat. Piranhas happily try and eat anything coming their way, so hooking them is not that hard, but it's advisable to use a metal leader as security. Also, don't leave shiny swivels farther up the line, because they will try and eat them too, usually cutting the line.

157
The monkey fish
Sucundurí River still water, Amazonas, Brazil
September to November
Silver arowana

The Sucundurí runs through some of the most beautiful and lush jungle in the Amazon. Far from civilization, the area around it is pristine and the wildlife is a joy to experience. The arowanas are famous for their ability to jump out of the water and snatch food from overhanging branches, several feet in the air—which has given them the nickname of "monkey fish." That is partly what draws anglers to target them, besides the fact that they are pretty fish, and fight with gusto even when airborne. Surface lures are preferred, and like many predators here, it helps if the bait is highly visible and makes an enticing noise.

156 | **A tooth-proof leader is essential for piranha**

157 | **Look out for the aerial antics of the silver arowana**

158 | **Amazon river dolphin**

158
Amazing catfish
Acarí River backwaters, Amazonas, Brazil
September to November
Reticulated shovelnose catfish (tiger catfish)

In a couple of places, the Acarí has areas of small islands with shallow water. These backwaters open up the jungle, where birds access the river more regularly. It is a spectacle of Amazon parrots, macaws, hoatzins, caracaras, and many other birds of prey; but also wonderful fishing-wise. The shovelnose catfish live here in big numbers. There are a few different species, but the most fascinating one is the reticulated shovelnose, or tiger catfish; for its combination of amazing looks, size, and fighting gusto. The shovelnose is a wary catfish, it doesn't just jump on the bait like many other catfishes. So it's much the sweeter when you finally hook this wonderfully striped cat.

159
Fishing with dolphins
Acarí River still water, Amazonas, Brazil
September to November
Southern peacock bass, freshwater barracuda, pike characin

The Acarí River runs fairly straight, and is not as winding as most other rivers in the system. It's generally deeper, too. The jungle around is as lovely and exotic here as in the rest of the system, however, there seems to be more visible wildlife, for example monkeys and river dolphins. Acarí is preferred by Brazilian anglers because of the large number of peacock bass and other fish species to catch on artificial baits like surface lures, wobblers, and big spinners. Most of these predator fish lurk right at the edge of the banks where jungle foliage overhangs, so that is where you want to put your baits.

160
Stingrays in freshwater
Sorubí River, Amazonas, Brazil
September to November
Ocellate river stingray

River stingrays are found all over South America, and the ocellate river stingray is the most prolific species. They live in fairly calm waters like river cut-offs, tidal lakes, and shallow river mouths, when the river is low. This species of river stingray grows to well over 70 lb (32 kg), but other closely related species grow even bigger. They are successful scavengers, not leaving any dead fish alone if possible, so it's not that hard to get a bite. They are good fun to catch, firstly because they take the bait very carefully so you have to be on top of your game when you strike, and then the fight is really something else, like fighting a tabletop.

161
Fast and furious
Sucundurí River fast water, Amazonas, Brazil
September to November
Payara, Amazon pellona

The Sucundurí River is one of the many tributaries of the Madeira River system, just south of Manaus. This river is bending and winding, and there are many little waterfalls and fast-water areas. These areas are great for various speedy and furious fish species, for example the Dracula of all fishes, the payara, or the Amazonian version of the tarpon, the pellona. These fish are highly active in the current, usually charging at anything resembling prey without reservations. Because of their mouths, they are very difficult to hook and keep on the hook, so large single hooks are advised, whether fishing with artificial or natural baits.

162
World's largest freshwater fish
Sucundurí River "lakes," Amazonas, Brazil
August to October
Arapaima

Arapaima is the world's largest solely freshwater fish, so what's not to like? However, it is not easy to find arapaima locations, and it is even harder to catch and land them. The arapaima prefers quiet and secluded areas of rivers, almost like small lakes. They hunt actively, and the whole jungle is awakened by the huge splashes as they chase prey, but they will just as eagerly take a dead-bait.

162 | **Tranquil waters attract arapaima**

163 | **The omnivorous blackfin pacu infest the Canumã River**

163
Nutty fish
Canumã River, Amazonas, Brazil
All year, but best April to October
Blackfin pacu (tambaqui), silver pacu
(pirapitinga)

At the quaint village of Foz do Canumã,
several small rivers enter the Canumã
River, and in this pristine area, deep in
the jungle, where the waters are calm and
trees overhang the river, you can catch the
plump, nut-eating pacu. The pacu are
known for their ability to crush nuts with
their human-like teeth, but they eat just
about anything they come across, such as
fruit, crustaceans, and other fish. The
easiest way to catch them is with a piece of
fish on a strong single hook, and then get
ready for an intensely hard fight.

164
Redtail action
Sucundurí River deep pools, Amazonas, Brazil
September to November
South American redtail catfish

The redtail catfish is widespread throughout
South America, and in the deep pools of the
Sucundurí River there are many very big, very
beautiful specimens. In the Sucundurí, there
are redtails of at least 100 lb (45 kg), and
considering that this species is not expected to
grow this big, it says something about this river.
The trick, when you fish for redtails, is to use
metal wire both before and after the lead, to
avoid having the line bitten through by
piranhas, who will almost always circle the bait;
but when all that is taken care of, you are in for
a fantastic fight, during which you can often
hear the catfish grunting underneath the boat.

165
Take part in world-class trout fishing
Warrah, Chartres, and Murrell Rivers, San Carlos, Falkland Islands
September to April
Brown trout, sea trout

The wild, rugged landscapes of the Falkland Islands offer some of the best sea trout fishing in the world. Northern brown trout were introduced to the island's oxygen-rich rivers in the 1940s and 1950s, and specimens of 10 lb (4.5 kg) are not uncommon (the record is a whopping 22 lbs 12.5oz (10.33 kg). The best months are September to October and February to March. Heavy rods are useful to cast your fly at a distance in windy conditions.

166
Dry-fly magic
Malleo River, Patagonia, Argentina
November to April
Brown trout, rainbow trout

The Malleo runs out of Tromen Lake and through a magical 50 mi (80 km) valley, rich in monkey-puzzle forests, wild rose bushes, red stags, wild hare, and fabulous trout. For many, the Malleo is in their top ten of dry-fly rivers in the world. Hatches of mayfly, caddis, and stonefly are abundant here. The river is a procession of riffles and pools and wading is relatively easy. It's the clarity of this ice-cold Andean river that inspires anglers to return annually, to a river where it is possible to stalk 8 lb (3.6 kg) browns in pristine surroundings.

165 | **Discover fly-fishing in the Falkland Islands with a guided trip**

167
BUCKET LIST FISH: Golden dorado
URUGUAY RIVER, URUGUAY

Don't be fooled by the golden halo around these dorado. Look into their mouths and you'll see the teeth of killers. These highly predatorial fish, closely related to the tigerfish of Africa, live in the rivers, lakes, and marshes of South America, notably Argentina, Bolivia, and Uruguay; the Uruguay River is one of the top locations. Fish of 20 lb (9 kg) are relatively common and 50 lb (22.5 kg) is a dream weight, but it is the savagery of the attack, often against surface-lures, and the fury of the fight, that makes them so prized. No wonder the fish is often called the giant trevally of freshwater.

Golden dorado are the swashbuckling pirates of freshwater, swaggering up the Uruguay River

168
Hitting the gold rush
Salto Grande Dam, La Zona, Uruguay River,
Uruguay/Argentina
May to August
Golden dorado

La Zona is a section of river beneath a dam where prey-fish gather in the millions and dorado congregate to enjoy the feast. The fishing is accessible but strictly controlled and that keeps pressure down. The result? Dorado mayhem. When La Zona is "on" it is described as the best freshwater lure-fishing in the world. Fish of 20 lb (9kg) are hardly glanced at, it's those of 40 lb (18 kg) which are the target. Sometimes the water visibly boils with striking dorado that simply hammer surface-lures.

170
Arrive by helicopter then enjoy remote fly-fishing
Chrome River, Los Lagos, Chile
February to April
Pacific salmon

If spotting your fish from the air sounds exciting, it's even better when you land in a place inaccessible to all others and start casting. Helicopter tours bring you right to the fish, often to places so remote you'll feel you're the first anglers to arrive there. Pacific salmon are the prime targets, but you can catch brook and rainbow trout as well. When you've fished out the spot you're at, just hop in the 'copter and it will whisk you away to another one.

169
Sea trout on fire
Rio Grande, Tierra del Fuego,
Argentina
January to April
Sea trout

Brown trout were introduced into the rivers of Tierra del Fuego in the 1930s and they thrived, especially in the Rio Grande. Today, more than 50,000 sea trout run this one river every season, with fish averaging 8 to 9 lb (3.6 to 4 kg) and ones of 20 lb (9 kg) caught with regularity. There's simply nowhere like it, but it is a big river and conditions are often challenging. Also on Tierra del Fuego, the Irigoyen River offers a smaller, more intimate experience where fish of 20 lb (9 kg) can be caught on 6 to 8wt gear. Which to choose, Grande or Irigoyen? It's a nice dilemma to have.

171
Fly-fish in translucent, jade-colored waters
Puelo River, Los Lagos, Chile
September to May
Brook trout, rainbows, chinook salmon

It's hard to find a more idyllic setting than the snow-capped peaks of Patagonia, the verdant forests, and the brilliant blue-green waters of the Puelo River. It is a prime habitat for rainbow trout, brook trout, and some of the world's largest chinook salmon. The lower third of the river, closest to the sea, has the densest populations, so catching great fish here is as close to a sure thing as most anglers can get.

171 | **A trip to the Puelo River will reward fly anglers**

172
Sighting gold
Agua Negra and Sécure Rivers,
Tsimané, Bolivia
June to mid-October
Golden dorado

This breathtaking national park
lies where the Amazon jungle
meets the Andes mountain
range. In the low-water season,
thousands of bait-fish make
their way up these river systems,
followed by prolific numbers
of large dorado. The upper
section of the Agua Negra is
a fly fisher's dream, all low, clear
water that offers unbelievable
sight-fishing for really big
dorado. The Securé is not far
behind, featuring large fish-
holding structures. You
can fish from dugouts or by
wading, casting for big fish in
what are little more than
mountain streams.

173
The jungle experience
Casaré River, Santa Cruz, Bolivia
June to October
Golden dorado

This is deep jungle fishing in territory that is incredibly
remote, reached by a two-and-a-half-hour flight from
Santa Cruz. Experience the terrific biodiversity of the
region while fishing small, intimate rivers for large
dorado. This is fly-fishing at its best, wading and sight-
fishing for groups of fish almost close enough to touch.
To get the best out of the adventure be prepared to stay
overnight in satellite camps. These will be basic but you'll
be fishing virgin water and be at one with the jungle.

174
Float down the Araza River to catch yatorana
Araza River, Peru
June to October
Yatorana

Rushing down from the misty Andes, the Araza River, a
tributary of the Inambari River near the village of Quince
Mil, is rich in nutrients, harboring a plethora of species,
including *salminus affinis*, known locally as dorada, and
yatorana, one of the strongest freshwater species out
there. Mainly feeding on fruits, insects, and small baitfish,
yatorana are extremely quick and always on the move
searching for schools of fish, making them the perfect
target for lure- and fly-anglers. You can also fly or spin fish
for rainbow trout in the surrounding mountain streams.

177 | Trout fishing in the Sacred Valley of the Incas is a unique experience

175
Formidable fighters

Iquitos, Amazon Basin, Peru

July to mid-October

Butterfly peacock bass

Butterfly bass are somewhat smaller than their bigger brothers and sisters, but even averaging 3 to 6 lb (1.4 to 2.7 kg) they fight like tigers rather than birds. Many a bent, size 4/0 hook will testify to that. From July to October the river is low and clean, and visibility is good for fly-fishing. Outfits of 6 to 8wt are recommended but leaders still need to be in the region of 16 lb (7.25 kg), preferably tapered mono. Employ flies that mimic small prey-fish—something flashy should work well.

176
A historic catch

Punta Sal, Tumbes, Peru

August, September, October

Black marlin

This area has been world-famous for its big-game fishing for years. Fish collect here because of a unique set of currents created by the meeting of the warm El Niño and cold Humbert waters. In addition to black marlin, there are striped marlin, wahoo, shark, tuna, barracuda, and dorado, among others. A world-record black marlin of 1,500 lb (680 kg) plus was caught, and it was the home of the Cabo Blanco Fishing Club made famous by Ernest Hemingway.

177
Trout at altitude

Sacred Valley Of The Incas, Cusco, Peru

April, June to October

Trout

This fishing adventure has real cultural appeal, especially if you are on a trip to Machu Picchu. There are high altitude lakes and rivers within two hours of Cusco, the imperial city of the Inca, which offer decent fly-fishing from boat and shore. The Apurimac River is cold and clear, as are several lakes lying at over 9,000 ft (2,743 m). The surrounding Andes offer a magnificent backdrop and you're likely to see llamas and alpacas close to the fascinating villages and farmsteads.

Track trout in the dramatic Cañete River

Peacock bass

Andean condor

178
Fish for trout in quiet pools and lagoons
Valley of Cañete, Peru
Mid-April to December
Rainbow trout

Flowing from the Andes to the Pacific, the Cañete River, south of Lima, provides excellent trout-fishing opportunities. Brought to Andean streams and rivers from Canada in 1939, rainbow trout can reach up to 18 in (46 cm), and are prized for their delicate flavor. Enjoy fly-fishing or spin-angling on the river's many lagoons and freshwater pools, and spot Andean wildlife too, including llamas, deer, monkeys, and condors.

A Galapagos tortoise shows the patience of an angler

The Galapagos sealion is evidence of the rich seas

Spectacular scenery and birdlife

A marlin shows why the species is so iconic

179
Bring your gear for spectacular marlin fishing
Galapagos Islands, Ecuador
All year, peak January to June
Blue, striped marlin

What angler doesn't dream of catching a mammoth marlin and wrestling it to the gunwales? The Galapagos is of course known for its incredible natural history and the discoveries of Charles Darwin, but its location out in the deep ocean makes it perfect for marlin fishing as well. It's common to catch (and release!) marlin in the 200 lb (90 kg) range, but some weighing 600 lb (270 kg) lurk in these magical depths. Keep fingers crossed and you'll be the next angler to land one!

180
Catch fish while endangered condors circle overhead
Highlands of Ecuador, El Cajas National Park, Cuenca, Ecuador
August to May
Rainbow trout

El Cajas National Park, near Cuenca, is a spectacular system of lakes, mountains, and streams that holds some of the world's largest and most beautiful rainbow trout. You'll likely spot endangered condors circling above as you fly-fish in mirror-like lakes and listen to the burble of rushing streams. Catching a rainbow here requires skill and patience, but those who come will be rewarded by impressive fish in an equally impressive landscape.

181
Glide through miles of protected wilderness
Oriente (Amazon) Jungle, Cuyabeno Wildlife Reserve, Ecuador
July to April
Rainbow bass

Known as *tucunare* in this region, rainbow bass of the Cuyabeno Wildlife Reserve are second to none. Land enormous fish while in one of Ecuador's most pristine, most remote, and most beautiful regions. Unlike the Brazilian side, the Ecuadorean region has superior infrastructure, meaning that journeying into this wilderness is not only faster, but safer as well.

180 | El Cajas is a wild and lovely place to fish

EUROPE

GREENLAND

186

183

182 184

185

190

189 188

187

ICELAND

191

192

FAROE

215

217

218

214

208–210

216 219 220

211

212

207

213

201–203, 206

204 199

205 198

197 200

295

294

296

276

277

278

301

302 298

305 304

299

303 300

308

292–293

306

307

284

291 289

287

286

285 282

283

290 297

281

279

280

242

243

244

245

222

246

247 248

241

236

237 239 240

238

224

288

AZORES

274

256

255

257

254 250 252

253

249

251

230

232

233

235

234

231

223

225

226

227

228

261 259

260 258

275

270–271 272

273

262

265 263

264

269 268 267 266

229

EUROPE: ENTRY LIST

182 | **The wolffish is a creature of the dark depths**

183 | **The Kangia is one of the great Arctic char rivers**

182
Devil fish
Fjords of Maniitsoq, Greenland
April to July
Atlantic wolffish, spotted wolffish

In Greenland, you have three species of wolffish. Two of these species, Atlantic and spotted wolffish, live in similar ways, in similar environments, and are more accessible to anglers, esepecially in spring, when they hunt for prey in the fjords and bays. In the Maniitsoq fjords, they can be caught in depths of up to 330 ft (100 m) and preferably over a sandy or muddy bottom. The wolffish are not exactly pretty, but they are impressive with toothy mouths, which can crush bones; and they are highly treasured as a food fish.

183
The valley from paradise
Kangia River, east coast of Greenland
July to September
Arctic char

These east-coast rivers are short, diamond-clear, and run from the Greenlandic ice cap to empty into the Davis Strait or the Baffin Sea. From early summer, rivers like the delightful Kangia are run by thousands of Arctic char seeking out their historic spawning grounds. These are electrifying fish, reaching 10 lb (4.5 kg) and resplendent in every color of the rainbow. You can fish fly or lure and search both the shallows and the pools. You live out of a tent. You walk miles in a day. You eat what you catch. It's the experience of a lifetime.

184
BUCKET LIST FISH: Arctic Char
ROBINSON RIVER, GREENLAND

Arctic char live worldwide in the cold seas and rivers above 64 degrees latitude, from Alaska east through Greenland, Iceland, Scandinavia, and Russia but also in the glacial lakes of Scotland and the Alps. Their close cousins, lake and brook trout, are found in North America but also in pockets worldwide where they have been introduced. The vibrant reds and oranges of the male Arctic char as it nears its spawning beds make it one of the most breathtaking of trophy fish.

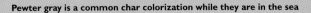

Pewter gray is a common char colorization while they are in the sea

185 | **Ice fishing feels unearthly**

186 | **A giant cod caught in a Greenland fjord**

185
Sleepy giant
Fjords of Maniitsoq, Greenland
Best March to April
Greenland sleeper shark

In the picturesque fjords of Greenland, with snow-capped mountains and azure blue water, you can catch the giant sleeper shark. These sharks mainly take slow-moving prey in the dark depths of the fjords, but they are also successful scavengers, with a taste for dead seals. Sleeper sharks roam in very deep water during summer, but venture closer to land in the colder months, and in April they are possible to catch both from ice-covered bays, or from boats. The best bait is a piece of smelly seal on a large shark-hook, fished above the bottom.

186
Inuit cod
Robinson River Bay, Greenland
April to August
Greenland cod

Robinson River is popular for its sea-running Arctic char-fishing. The estuary is large and enclosed, and usually protected from the harsh Arctic winds; there the cod hunt in the spring and summer. From an angler's point of view, Greenland cod are similar to their Pacific and Atlantic cousins in most ways; how to catch them, how they fight, and how they look. They can be caught from shore, if you let a heavy spinner or spoon drop a few feet down, or from a boat using pirks (spoon-like lures) at any depth to about 160 ft (50 m). Many anglers recommend replacing the treble hook for a single hook.

187 | **The untamed rivers of Iceland stir the soul of any angler**

187
Land of ice, fire, and salmon

Iceland
**June to September (but check
local seasons)**
Atlantic salmon

There are more than one hundred top
salmon rivers in Iceland, including the West
Ranga, the Laxá, the Fossá, the Grímsá, and
the Sog, and virtually all of them offer an
intimate, visual experience. Many of the
rivers are small and allow opportunities for
7/8 and even 6wt gear. They tend to be clear
so sight-fishing is possible and small flies on
floating lines work well. The so-called "white
nights of summer," when the sun doesn't set,
encourage fishing early and late in the day
(or night) and you can fish stunning
landscapes in perfect peace.

188
Take 100 yards of backing

Lake Þingvallavatn, Reykjavik, Iceland
April to September
Brown trout

At 32 sq mi (83 sq km) this is the largest
natural lake in Iceland, set in its own
national park, and listed as a UNESCO
World Heritage Site. Everything here is
special including the four varieties of Arctic
char, some of which are the prey of the
colossal wild brown trout living here. At
20 or even 30 lb (9 to 13 kg), these are the
largest browns in the world so tackle up
accordingly—yes, you'll need 100 yds (91 m)
of backing! The lake is crystal-clear so
sight-fish along the crevasses, or fish dry flies
in the shallow bays. In the months of 24-hour
daylight, twilight is the top fishing time.

189
BUCKET LIST
FISH: Halibut
ICELAND

This mammoth flatfish exists in the deepest, darkest, coldest chasms of the North Atlantic and Pacific Oceans. Here you can locate them at depths of 800 ft (245 m) where they can grow to a staggering 800 lb (360 kg) or more. It's a fascinating fish. Some adults are true nomads and in a single year have been known to travel 2,000 mi (3,220 km) in search of food. Halibut fishing is not for the faint-hearted. You have to expect cold weather and stormy seas. Your bait will be taken at a vast depth and then the war between fish and angler begins: an enormous fish and an enormous challenge.

Much of the life of the enormous halibut is secret, hidden in the uncharted depths of the ocean

190
Relaxed Reykjavik fishing
Reykjavik, Iceland
May to September
Halibut, cod, pollock

Not all adventures have to be full-on, demanding challenges. It is possible to take boat expeditions from the old harbor in Reykjavik that are simply all about fun fishing and often very productive. Largely because of Iceland's progressive conservation policies there are many, many fish out there, so some companies offer a complimentary trip if you fail to catch anything. Gear and warm clothing is generally supplied, and fishing begins shortly after leaving port. The chance of seeing puffins only adds to the experience.

191
Jaws in unpredictable waters
Mykines Coast and Vestmanna Fjord,
Faroe Islands
**November to February, but best
November and February**
Porbeagle shark

Both the waters and the weather around this North Atlantic archipelago and island country, are notoriously unpredictable, but the fishing is second to none in so many ways. One is the porbeagle shark, which visits in winter. The porbeagle is targeted either by anchoring up, chumming, and fishing with fish-bait under a balloon, or by trolling with huge jigs. The average size of porbeagle here is 154 to 330 lb (70 to 150 kg).

190 | **A sighting of the Northern Lights enhances any trip**

191 | **The Faroe Islands offer huge rewards**

192
The wild heart of sea fishing
Faroe Islands/Sorvagurfjord
May to October
Ling, pollock, cod, whiting

There's nowhere like the Faroes, eighteen islands that are the tips of a vast underwater mountain range off the coast of Scotland. This leads to depths of 2,625 ft (800 m) plus just off-shore, and water where the cold polar seas mingle with the warmth of the Gulf Stream. These happy chances of geography create one of the most fertile sea-fisheries in the world. You can fish from shore or a boat but the uniqueness of the adventure lies in the unspoiled wilderness that is home to a puffin paradise.

193
The biggest flatfish on the planet
Norway
April to September
Halibut

Marks such as Sandland Brygge, Havøysund, and the Lofoten Archipelago give access to some of the most pulsating deep-sea fishing on the planet. We are talking halibut: fish bigger than you are, the monster flatfish of the northern seas. You can bait-fish for halibut but many prefer lure-fishing, intercepting these bottom feeders when they come into midwater and above to feed. Then the fun begins as the enraged creatures dive for the rocky bed with colossal power. Thus begins an epic battle between fisher and fish with a backdrop of towering cliffs, sea eagles, and the amazing sunsets of a pristine world.

194

Giants of the frozen seas
Sørvaer, Sørøya, Norway
March and April
Cod

This adventure is not for the timid; simply getting as far north as the island of Sørøya, way above the Arctic Circle, is a trek in itself. The weather is fearsomely ferocious in March and April, and the cold penetrating. You are fishing afloat, often in waves of 6 ft (1.8 m) or more, on the drift, working long back-breaking lures at colossal depths. However, the cod are huge; sometimes a staggering 60 lb (27 kg) plus. Catch and release is the norm, so the fish have to be levered from the depths with agonizing slowness, and they have to be netted and returned with care.

195

River of "fifties"
Alta River, Norway
June to August
Atlantic salmon

Royalty and rock stars have traditionally fished the mighty Alta, paying excruciatingly high rates each day for the privilege. However, there is also a way to fish from its hallowed banks if you enter the famous Alta River Lottery that gives you the chance of 36 hours in this salmon paradise. Every year, fish of 50 lb (22.5 kg) are taken on the fly and "thirties" and over are commonplace. This is a remote river in the north of the country and it is a surreal experience to catch huge fish in scenery of magical beauty at the time of the midnight sun.

192 | **Make the most of the solitude in the Faroe Islands**

Cod grow from this to ten times the size

196
BUCKET LIST FISH: Cod
NORWAY

For centuries, cod has been the most important fish on both sides of the North Atlantic. The deep, cool waters of Norway are food-rich for the massive cod that live there. Commercial overfishing is a problem, but sport-anglers are still catching these bronzed beauties up to 50 lb (22.5 kg) and more, especially in the deeper, colder waters farther north. Use fish baits for these fish, or better still use heavy metal pirks (spoon-like lures) that allow you to get deep to where the true monsters lurk. In heavy weather, on a rolling sea, bringing a giant cod up from the depths is a true test for any angler.

197 | **For heart-stopping sport garfish are hard to beat**

197

Grand garfish
Øresund, Denmark/Sweden
May to August
Garfish

Øresund is the picturesque strait between Denmark and Sweden, at the entrance to the Baltic Sea. Every spring and fall, Øresund is host to enormous numbers of garfish, which migrate to the Baltic Sea to spawn, and then return to Skagerrak and the North Sea in the fall. The garfish attack baits readily, but the tricky bit is to land them. Their long, toothy beaks are difficult to set a hook into, so use stinger treble hooks on slender spoons, or silk thread (but no hook), which entangles their many teeth. Alternatively, you can catch them using small filets of herring or shrimp under a float. The garfish is a favorite because of its fighting qualities, aerobatics, and tail-dancing.

198
Zander magnet
Skanderborg Lake, Jutland, Denmark
Spring to fall (No zander fishing in May)
Zander

This is a spectacular lake surrounded by forests and fringed by reed-beds. It lies close to the town of the same name, a charming place to visit or stay. The lake itself is renowned for zander, reputedly the best venue in the country. Smaller fish up to 7 lb (3 kg) are relatively easy but the lake has produced fish in excess of 22 lb (10 kg). Spring and fall see the zander hunting in the shallows but the heat of summer drives them deeper into the center of the lake where you need a boat to pursue them successfully.

199
Fish in the city
Island of Zealand, Copenhagen, Denmark
Winter and spring
Perch

There cannot be another capital city so rich in fishing locations. Copenhagen sits between the North and the Baltic Seas and is rich in sea trout and cod but also boasts terrific sport for pike and perch. Because the Baltic is mildly brackish, you'll find big perch along the shorelines, in the beach-parks of Amager, as well as in the streams in the east of the island, south of the capital. There are plenty of lakes too, including Damhus, Sorø, and Esrum. It's a terrific perch location, close to one of the most exciting cities in Europe.

199 | **Visit Amager beach-park for the chance to catch perch**

200
Lengths of silver
Bornholm Island, Denmark
Mid-September to late May
Sea trout

This island lives for fishing, and its shores offer a fabulous experience. The sea retains some warmth through the winter and the salinity levels are low, both factors in attracting feeding fish. Spawning streams and strict regulations mean stocks remain high. Fishing demands hard work for massive rewards, sometimes in the shape of a 10 lb (4.5 kg) plus fish. Lures and flies both catch fish and there are spits, reefs, rocks, and underwater structures to target. Local tackle shops are very helpful if you need advice.

201
Winter guest
Suså River, Sjælland, Denmark
December to February
European whitefish

Romantic Suså River has much to offer: canoeing, picnicking along its banks, as well as the various fish species which have a tendency to reach big sizes and good numbers there. One of the more special fish species is the whitefish, which makes its spawning run in winter, and is best fished in places with a strong current, not too far from the estuary. The whitefish are caught either on flies, both wet and dry, or more easily float-fished with a waggler and a small hook with a couple of maggots.

202
Bream everywhere
Suså River, Sjælland, Denmark
All year, but best May to September
Common bream

You can find bream just about everywhere in Denmark, but in the rivers—particularly the Suså—you'll find fish of serious sizes. In the deep parts, near the estuary, the bream compete with carp for food. Often you'll catch bream while carp fishing, but when you target the bream themselves, it is not only more fun to fight them, but the biggest ones can be lured with big earthworms.

203
Rivers of pike
Tryggevælde River and Tude Å River, Sjælland, Denmark
February to October, but closed season is March 15 to April 30
Northern pike

The good-sized rivers here all hold nice-sized pike. Of course, there are many small ones, but to isolate the bigger fish, use big live- or dead-baits, suspended just over the bottom, and under overhanging trees or up against the reeds, in the deepest parts. Pike from 11 to 26 lb (5 to 12 kg) can be caught here.

204

Chasing gray ghosts

Samsø Island, Jutland Peninsula, Denmark

May to October

Gray mullet

Mullet are almost ghost-like—one of the most difficult of fish to tempt with any bait or fly but it can be done here at Samsø Island. This is a lovely place to visit in the spring and summer—very serene—with waves of mullet following the tides. There are beaches, jetties, and shallow lagoons that attract the mullet and you can fish for them with pinches of bread-flake on small hooks and float-tackle. Fly-fishing is gaining in popularity and different experts all swear by different patterns—a good bet is to try something small and green.

204 | **No wonder mullet are known as "gray ghosts," they must escape many predators**

206 | The zander is a cunning fish that attracts anglers who are dedicated to catching it

205

Flat and dramatic

Jutland, Denmark

April to September

Common turbot

Jutland's west coast is dramatic and very beautiful. The stretch between Blåvandshuk and Nymindegab is believed to have the best turbot spots, and there are many. The turbot is a big flatfish, one of the biggest, when you exclude halibut. But it is very different from other flatfish, which are usually found in fairly deep water. The turbot hunts in shallow water, as low as 20 in (50 cm), even though it grows quite big. You can use compact spoons with a leader to a piece of fish.

206

The place for big zander

Fureso Lake, Sjælland, Denmark

All year, but closed season is May, best June to July

European zander

The best place to fish big zander in Denmark is the large and deep Fureso Lake. Fureso is surrounded by natural forest and beautiful private houses. In spring, you can catch the zander within casting distance from shore where they congregate to spawn, making the males extra aggressive. At that point you can catch them on either slow-moving Rapalas or on float-fished bait-fish. In summer, fall, and winter they are found in the depths of the lake and are best caught on vertical jigging, fished just above the bottom. The local record is just over 20 lb (9 kg), with many fish between 4 and 10 lb (1.8 and 4.5 kg).

207
Baltic crocodiles
Baltic Archipelago at Trosa, Västervik, and
Maraviken, Sweden
March to April; September to October
Northern pike

The coast here is riddled with archipelagos
where big pike live; big, as in 33 to 45 lb (15
to 20 kg) plus. In April, they congregate near
the reedy shorelines in preparation for
spawning, it is then that pike-fishing here is
world class. In September and October, the
pike are caught mostly in the open sea. The
best bait in spring are medium-sized jigs with
a stinger treble hook, fished right to the
edge of the reeds. In fall, any standard pike
bait will do, such as Rapalas, spoons, and
spinner-baits; pike-flies often work brilliantly.

208
Ice-age fish
Jämtland, Sweden
All year
Whitefish

The beautiful landscape of Jämtland is
dotted and crisscrossed with lakes and rivers.
In this wild and wonderful place, among
reindeer and moose, you will find a number
of elusive species of whitefish, some of which
were landlocked after the last ice age; for
example, the lacustrine fluvial whitefish in
Gunnarvattnet Lake, the maraena whitefish
in Indalsälven River, and the Valaam
whitefish in Locknesjön Lake. The whitefish
are feisty salmonids and are very tasty; both
the meat, and especially the roe, which is
world class and very expensive.

209

Grayling dream

Kvissle River, Jämtland, Sweden

June to August, but best at end of June

Grayling

Kvissle River is a part of the great Indalsälven River, which runs from the huge Storsjön Lake to the Baltic. Kvissle is considered to be one of Sweden's best grayling waters. Fishing from land is easy enough, but if you're prepared to do some wading in the rocky current you have so many more spots to explore. You can fish the grayling with small spinners, dry flies, and bead head nymph flies. The population of grayling in this system is phenomenal, with normal catches of 1 to 2 lb (0.45 to 0.9 kg) fish, and yearly catches of grayling of over 4.4 lb (2 kg).

208, 209 | **Jämtland is a forgotten wilderness**

210 | **Enjoy the vast waters and trout at Storsjön Lake**

210
Big water, big fish
Storsjön Lake, Jämtland, Sweden
June to August
Lake trout

One of Sweden's many gigantic lakes, Storsjön, houses a healthy population of lake trout weighing up to 22 lb (10 kg) and more. Because the water is so vast, the most effective way to fish for them is by trolling, to cover as much area and depth as possible. You can catch them on classic multicolored trolling spoons, and you will rarely have a fishing day without strong fighting fish between 2 and 9 lb (0.9 and 4 kg).

211
Discover gold in the forests
Lake Ursjön, Sweden
July and August
Crucian carp

There is something magical about fishing this shallow, crystal-clear lake in the midst of a Swedish forest. Fishing access is limited so tranquility is assured and you can worship at the altar of the biggest crucian carp in the world. It's normal to catch 3 to 4 lb (1.4 to 1.8 kg) fish and "sixes" are possible but best of all, they behave like crucians should: they bubble and roll on the surface and fall for small baits, fished close-in under a float. Big bags are not frequent but Ursjön is the place where dreams are made.

212

Monster mayhem

Baltic Sea

All year, but observe regional closed seasons; pike, commonly March and April

Sea trout, pike

The Baltic Sea is simply an angling "must fish" for the trophy-seeker. It's almost too immense to single out a species, but sea trout and pike must come top of a list that includes salmon, perch, and zander too. The reason for the huge specimens found here lies in the fact that the brackish water is extremely fertile, rich in shrimp, crab, and smaller prey-fish. Hotspots include Swedish Gotland, the Stockholm Archipelago, and Rügen Island on the German Baltic coast.

213

Sixties from the sea

The Archipelago of Sweden

April to October

Pike

The world's biggest pike swim in the Baltic Sea along Sweden's east coast where the water is just brackish enough for this freshwater species to survive. Think monsters of 60 lb (27 kg), perhaps more. In April, the colossal female fish come inshore to spawn in the reed-filled bays. Through the summer and into the fall, they move out to the islands just off the coast where they ambush passing schools of herring and cod, and grow even bigger. Fish with big lures from a boat, and watch out for the leviathans in clear water!

212 | **The brackish waters of the Baltic are food-rich and home to sea trout and pike of unbelievable size**

214

A wilderness rarity

Skivsjo Lake, Sweden
May to October
Burbot

This is a slightly odd adventure, as the burbot is one of the less glamorous targets in this book. However, it has achieved a near cult status in the UK, especially over the years it has become rare to the point of extinction there. The good news is that the species is alive and thriving in this distant Swedish stronghold. Skivsjo is a beautiful lake, 5 mi (8 km) long and surrounded by moose-filled forests. The burbot keep to the bed and can be caught on dead baits but also jigging plastic lures. They won't pull your arm off but they have a strange mottled beauty to them and a plethora of coloration from yellow to a deep blue and everything in between.

215

Delights of the Arctic Circle

Lapland, Finland
July and August
Arctic Char

Char are the most dramatic of targets, often called the "Garbo" of fish because of their beauty and unpredictability. The northernmost areas of Sweden offer true adventures for these explosive fish that can exceed 10 lb or even 20 lb (4.5 or 9 kg) in weight. Most anglers fly-fish in the lakes and rivers here, and sometimes the tiniest midge pattern will take the biggest fish. You might be bank-fishing, wading, even float-tubing, and all this takes place in and around the ancestral lands of the Sami people whose culture and existence is based around the prolific reindeer in this remote region.

216

The smash and grab predator of the North

Kokemäenjoki River and its tributary Loimijoki, Finland
Late June to September
Asp

If you haven't ever considered asp-fishing then think again. These are super-charged chub, similar in looks but bigger and way more ferociously predatorial. The Finnish rivers are lonely and beautiful, a challenge in themselves, and when asp are on the prowl watch out for fireworks. Asp hunt small fish in packs, driving them to the surface where they hit them hard. Watch for top-water eruptions and fish a plug, spoon, spinner, or rubber through the commotion—a truly amazing summer-angling experience.

A reindeer sighting creates a sense of adventure

Sunset at Oulanka National Park

The glorious colors and spotting of an arctic grayling

217
Enjoy this wilderness
Lapland, Finland
Summer and fall
Grayling

Lapland, in the north of Finland, offers some of the greatest grayling adventures on the planet. Rivers like the Teno and the Tornionjoki produce huge fish in excess of 3 lb (1.4 kg). But perhaps the greatest, toughest test of all is to trek in the Oulanka National Park, fishing this east Lapland wilderness as you go. The Aventojoki and the Savinajoki are just two of the rushing streams that produce wonderful fish. See reindeer and red squirrels, and eat wild mushrooms or blueberries as you camp in this exquisite place. You'll marvel at where your rod can lead you.

218

Lapland delight
Børgefjell, Lapland (Norway/Sweden)
June to September
Brown trout

Børgefjell, on the border of Norway and Sweden, boasts some of the best landscape that either country can offer, with stunning wildlife and flora. The streams and small lakes here contain a special kind of brown trout, which hasn't mixed with any other strain since the last ice age. They don't grow big, but they are beautiful and hard fighters. They happily take any kind of spinner, small lure, spoon, and all manner of flies, as these waters are sparse with food. There are always happy days with a good many specimens.

218 | Børgefjell is an untouched wilderness

219

The ferocious predator of the north

Lake Kulovesi and Siuronkoski Rapids,
Nokia, Finland
Late June to September
Asp

Asp have had their problems over recent years but seem to be making a strong recovery in some Finnish locations. This is excellent as the asp is a great fish, rather like a large, violently predatorial chub. Catch them on spinners, spoons, large streamer flies, and fish baits. Watch out for dramatic surface eruptions as packs of asp come in to feed on small fish and then get after them fast. These Finnish locations are strong, but the asp situation is a fluid one in northern Europe and some Swedish rivers are showing potential too.

220

Mystery under the ice

Lake Päijänne, Finland
December to April
Burbot, perch

Päijänne is large, popular, and one of the most pristine waters in Europe. It is rich in fish-stocks and throughout the year predator-fishing is extremely good. Summer sees big catches of roach, bream, and ide. You can even target that rare white fish: the vendace. In winter, the ice-fishing is a major event and snowmobiles crisscross the frozen vastness. Winter is the time to target perch, but burbot is also a cold-weather favorite. You can fish the lake for the price of a National Fishing Management Fee, but when it comes to ice-sport it's worth using a guide who knows the terrain. Better safe than sorry.

219 | **The Finnish asp is a thrilling target**

220 | **Lake Päijänne is home to burbot**

A big, dark Lapland grayling has predatorial habits and is happy to take a spinner

221
BUCKET LIST FISH: Grayling
EASTERN EUROPE

These beautiful fish exist throughout the entire northern hemisphere, wherever the waters are cold, clean, and high in oxygen. There are many local strains of this graceful fish, perhaps in excess of thirty, and some varieties in Central Asia have only recently been identified. In many Eastern European countries, grayling are prized as highly as trout, and no wonder. They can be caught on dry flies, nymphs, bait—and even small spinners in places like Lapland where the bigger fish become predatorial.

222
World-class dry fly-fishing
San River, Poland
May to September
Trout and grayling

This is one of the great fly destinations of Europe. It rises in the Carpathian Mountains and flows southeast toward Ukraine. Angling first took notice in 1985 when the World Fly-fishing Championships were held here. The most exhilarating way to fish here is to wade upriver, casting dry flies 20 yds (18 m) ahead of you. Pristine trout and grayling appear from nowhere and you can hear the take echo in the deep silence of the forest.

223
Flood city
Raduta Lake, Sarulesti, Romania
All year
Grass carp, common carp

The Raduta Lake is really a flooded area, where once stood villages and fields. It now looks like any lakeside landscape. The lakes are huge carp, zander, and sturgeon fisheries. The fishery provides everything from tackle and bait, to boats, and food delivered on the bank. The fishing potential is enormous, with carp in world-record sizes, and grass carp in beast size. They are caught with the standard carp methods: rod pods and hard-boiled bait.

224
Carp dreamland
Island and Heaven lakes, Hungary
Spring to fall
Carp

Eastern Europe has become a carper's paradise these last few years and there are no two better lakes to start on than Heaven and Island. All lakes have their own character but these two are similar in being very large, very beautiful, and full of big fish—expect 40 to 50 lb (18 to 22.5 kg) for sure. Hungary is worth the visit for its lovely people and gentle pace of life. When the weather is good, there is no better place on earth, and the carp are equally special.

222 | **The San River is one of central Europe's great game-fish destinations**

226 | A wild carp

227 | Greek rivers like the Acheron are home to trout

225
A kaleidoscope of beauty

The four seas, Turkey
September to January
Sea species

Turkey offers very special saltwater-fishing indeed. It is bordered by four seas—the Mediterranean Sea, the Black Sea, the Aegean Sea, and the Marmara Sea. And, as if that's not enough, there are also the wonderful waters of the Dardanelles and the Bosporus. Although September to January is best, there is generally at least one species in season all year. All the iconic fish swim the Turkish coast but there are also unique opportunities for Marmara perch, Black Sea bass, or Black Sea salmon.

226
Ancient carp adventure

Lake Volvi, Thessaloniki, Greece
May to September
Wild carp

So-called "wild carp" are really fully scaled common carp that owe their origins to a time before carp cultivation. They are long, lean, fight ferociously, and have achieved some measure of cult status because of their rarity. Volvi is a huge lake, 12 mi (19 km) long, 6 mi (10 km) or more wide and, until recently at least, wild carp were netted commercially. The perch-fishing is reputedly good and there are supposedly catfish present in this beautiful lake.

227
Trout amid the olive groves

The Epirus region, northern Greece
Late spring to early fall
Brown trout

This mountainous region is famed for its rivers, notably the Louros and the Acheron. They tumble cold and crystalline through oak-clad mountain sides which are redolent in antiquity. You could find yourself casting a fly into the eddies created by a Roman aqueduct built 2,000 years ago. In fact, it is highly likely that this is where fly-fishing was born, in the second century AD. These rivers are hard to fish but a real challenge in the shadow of the Classical Age.

228

Fascinating sport, breathtaking backdrops

Coastline of Greece

Summer

Mullet, sea bream

This adventure is all about fun and simple pleasures. Greece possesses an 8,000 mi (12,875 km) coastline and most of it offers superb angling opportunities. You don't need a license, just some basic gear like a travel rod, floats, hooks, a few light lures, and perhaps a loaf or two of bread. The bread is for mullet in the many harbors, and the rubber lures and plugs for bream and wrasse anywhere you see a few rocks emerging from the crystal seas. Stunning scenery, glorious weather, and fishing that is fast and furious.

228 | The Greek coastline is steeped in beauty and offers exhilarating sport

229 | **Trolling the prolific Tyrrhenian Sea**

230 | **The crystal waters of the Sarca river**

229

A Mediterranean treasure-trove

Cagliari, Sardinia, Italy

May to October

Bluefin tuna

The deep waters of the Tyrrhenian Sea between Sardinia and Sicily are an often overlooked sea-fishing paradise. Amberjack, grouper, and snapper are just three species out of many that are prolific here. Bass and sea-bream fishing can be thrilling closer into town, as is the run of gigantic bluefins that makes the area so special. They arrive at the start of the summer and can be big; the most common method is trolling with sardine-type baits. And don't miss out on the historic and cultural delights of this island's capital.

230

Exquisite beauty, awesome size

Sarca River, Trento, Italy

Mid-April to October

Marble trout

There is a good reason why the 2019 World Fly-fishing Championship was held on the Sarca. This is a powerful river that really challenges any angler. All top methods work well and the undoubted prime target is the famed marble trout, one of the great challenges in the fly world. They grow big here and fight hard in cold, muscular water. The breathtaking scenery is a bonus, as are frequent captures of intensely beautiful char species.

231 | **Mean, moody, full of menace, the pike really does stir the blood**

231
BUCKET LIST FISH: Pike
SALTO AND ISCO LAKES, ITALY

Pike are the most angled-for freshwater predator in the northern hemisphere. They are present through much of Europe, North America, and east to Siberia. The mighty muskellunge is a purely North American member of the family just as the Amur pike is restricted to the very far east of Mongolia, Siberia, and the borders of China. Pike reach 50 lb (22.5 kg) and "muskies" perhaps almost double that weight, and all have teeth to match. Dead-baiting and lure-fishing are the most common approaches and learning sound unhooking practices is essential.

232

Glacial giants

Glacial lakes, north Italy

All year, but check local closed seasons

Pike

Put simply, lakes like Bracciano, El Salto, Iseo, and Centro Cadore hold staggering pike. Firstly, they can be huge, 50 lb (22.5 kg) plus is always possible. Secondly, these pike are awe-inspiring to look at. Their markings are leopard-like in their boldness and the colorations vary wildly—there's even a strain that displays deep-red or crimson fins. Most fishing is done from boats, often with big rubber lures and heavy jig-heads to get down deep. In cold, crystal water the fight of these fish is pulsating, enough to divert you from the glorious Alpine scenery all around.

233

Thrilling fly-fishing

Soča River, Slovenia

April to October

Wild rainbow trout, marble trout, Adriatic grayling

This stunning, green-tinged river rises in the Julian Alps and runs through a landscape of forests and mountains. The fish reflect the wild beauty of their environment and the fly-fishing here is some of the most exhilarating in the world. The Soca is all about stealth, delicacy, and precision. The marble trout are the ultimate trophy here, a strain of fish unique to the rivers of the Adriatic basin. They grow to 20 lb (9 kg) or more and the battle in a river so fast, so rock strewn, is indescribable.

233 | Mountains, forests, crystalline water, and marble trout—you must fish the Sŏca river if you can

234

Sharp-toothed salmon of Slovenia

Sava Bohinjka River, Slovenian Alps, Slovenia

October to mid-February

Huchen

The huchen is a cousin of the mighty Asian taimen and can grow to a whopping 100 lb (45 kg). The fish is sometimes called the Danubian salmon as it lives in the rivers of the Danubian Basin and is a strain of landlocked salmon. Whatever its name, this is the most prized quarry throughout central and eastern Europe for its size, rarity, and ferocity. The Sava and its huchen-rich tributaries like the Krka flow transparent green in color, past picture-postcard villages and churches, and as the snow falls they become places of wonder. Fish big flies or lures early and late when the frost bites.

235

There's nothing gray about these fish

Unec River, Slovenia

May to November

Adriatic grayling

There are innumerable sub-species and strains of grayling around the world and for many fly connoisseurs they are every bit as desirable as brown trout. Some of the most flamboyant in coloring are the Adriatics— glorious grayling found in several eastward-flowing Slovenia rivers. The Unec is a top location, stunning like all these Alpine rivers and renowned for grayling rising to the dry fly. This river can suffer from low water levels in the summer, but there are alternative rivers close by, so sport is pretty much guaranteed.

236

Casting close to heaven

Goiserer Traun River, near Hallstatt, Austria

May to December

Grayling

There are marvelous grayling rivers in Austria but this has to be one of the best. Grayling of 18 in (46 cm) and more are caught here and the fishing gets better as fall advances. By September, the water is at its clearest and shines with a slight green tinge. Then huge fish can be stalked, using the French-leader technique that has revolutionized grayling fishing this century. This is a protected area and the fishing is highly regulated to keep pressure to a minimum. The wildlife and the scenery are both as spectacular as the fishing.

235 | **The Alpine scenery of the Unec river is a joy**

236 | **The Goiserer Traun offers grayling fishing**

237
Monsters in the mountains
Drau River, Hohe Tauern National Park, Austria
Winter
Alpine salmon

The giant Alpine salmon are essentially huchen, successfully introduced into this angler's paradise of forests, mountains, glaciers, and waterfalls. Running through the landscape is the magnificent Drau River, in winter a fearsome sight. Heavy rains and snowmelt only up the challenge, but the rewards are huge. Big lures, heavy flies, and gear strong enough to land 40 lb (18kg) fish in a torrent is what this game is about. Definitely one of the great angling adventures of the world.

238
Fishing in a pristine world
Gail River, Lesachtal Valley, Austria
April to October
Rainbow trout

Many would say the Gail is the most exquisite of all the rivers in the Austrian Alpine region, and certainly its clear waters are of drinking quality. The mesmerizing valley itself features deep gorges, forests, and alpine meadows, often spangled with wild flowers. Six tributaries flow into the main river and this creates a wide variety of water to fish. Fly-fishing for brown trout and grayling is also of the highest quality and many of the latter reach 3 lb (1.4 kg) in weight. Focus on rainbows though, because the crystal waters of the Gail paints them in colors beyond compare.

237 | **The River Drau holds Europe's biggest huchen**

238 | **A trout is unhooked in the water**

Huchen—and their larger relatives, the taimen, shown here—are a savage challenge

239
BUCKET LIST FISH: Huchen and taimen
GERMANY, AUSTRIA, AND SLOVENIA

Huchen and taimen are predominantly freshwater, salmon-like species and are closely related. The huchen is, perhaps, the biggest prize for any angler in Eastern Europe, and its larger relative, the taimen, can be found throughout Siberia, Russia, Mongolia, and even the far west of China. A seriously large huchen can reach 50 to 60 lb (22.5 to 27 kg) and there are well-founded stories of taimen double that weight. The real importance of these fish, however, lies in their rarity and their ferocious lure-attacks and fighting ability in tumultuous rivers. These fish reflect the wild terrain they inhabit. These are extraordinary beasts and have been caught on dead squirrels, rat lures, and dead birds drifted downstream.

240
Simply awesome challenge
River Danube
Winter
Huchen

The mighty Danube is the spiritual home of the huchen, also known as the Danubian salmon. In this huge river, location is first and foremost. Fishing is largely a winter occupation when the fish do not show themselves, so investigate rocks, islands, and built structures which are huchen-magnets. Colossal huchen have become recognized, targeted, and almost deified by the lure-anglers who pursue them. Taking a winter huchen from the Danube is one of Europe's top five challenges.

241
Water clear as air
Black Forest Creeks, Germany
April to September
Trout

Ernest Hemingway, the ultimate angling explorer, traveled hereabouts in the 1920s and ran up against the authorities, but if you get your licenses, there is lovely fly-fishing in rivers like the Hauensteiner Alb, the Kleine Kinzig, and the Murg. Many of the streams in the area run into the Upper Rhine and are crystal-clear following deep, tree-clad valleys. This is a picture-postcard setting with waterfalls, rapids and pools, shrines, and pretty villages with inns for the tired angler.

240 | The Danube's population of the exotic huchen is second to no other river

242
A country of opportunities
Canals, rivers, and lakes, the Netherlands
January to March, September to December
Zander

The Netherlands has to be Europe's top zander destination, and there are so many locations it is hard to pin a best one down. So-called "street-fishing" in the canals of Amsterdam and Rotterdam and the murky water of the Waal and Hollands Diep allows you to catch them in the daytime—zander are notoriously difficult in bright light. You can jig, troll, or try bottom fishing but remember these are cunning fish. Using a guide is a shortcut to the best areas.

242 | **The canals of the Netherlands offer endless opportunities to catch fish, notably the zander**

243
Six-pound striped warriors
Lake Oostvoorne, the Netherlands
Winter months
Perch

It is hard to isolate any one of the Netherlands's gigantic perch waters. Many are large lakes, like Oostvoorne, but there are canals, such as Voorne, and rivers and drains everywhere. The key is to find the bait fish and then work rubber lures, mostly jig heads, carefully up and down the water column. This can be grueling in winter but the rewards are awesome. These are perch of 6 lb (2.7 kg) or more, perhaps the biggest you'll be able to find in Europe.

244
The canal's gentle giant
Ghent-Terneuzen Canal, Holland/Belgium
Summer
Ide

This 20 mi (32 km) long canal flows between Belgium and Holland and was built in the 1800s to transport cargo. It is wide and deep and full of unexpected fish, notably the ide, but you can also catch everything from eels to mullet and flounder here. Ide are very roach-like and grow to around 5 lb (2.3 kg) or so. The species is active in the summer months, particularly at dusk and into the night. The canal is too big to fly-fish successfully so a bait-approach is best.

245

A big fish destination

Timmy's Lake, Geel, Belgium

All year, although slow in winter

Carp

Timmy's is a carp complex much loved by its regulars. There are around a dozen acres (4.8 hectares) of water lying on a small estate and the swims are tree-lined and scenic. The water is relatively shallow so there is good weed-growth and plenty of features to fish around. The whole venue is tremendously well set up: you can drive to your chosen pitch, there are cabins, showers, and meals delivered to the bank. Above all, there are big numbers of big carp in the 30 to 50 lb (13 to 22.5 kg) range, all good looking and in splendid condition. A warm welcome and as much advice as you might want complete a great package.

246

Eiffel Tower action

The Seine, Paris, France

May to January

Catfish, carp, perch

Back in the 1970s, the Seine was hideously polluted. Today it is a rich fishery and much enjoyed by visitors and locals alike. Younger people especially are enjoying the delights of modern drop-shotting for perch, which is great sport and mobile. Specialist anglers are targeting big carp and serious catfish in the very shadows of landmarks like the Eiffel Tower and Notre Dame Cathedral. Boat-traffic can become disruptive during the day, so early and late can see the best sport, but do remember night-fishing has been illegal here since 1669.

245 | A huge carp is unhooked with utmost care

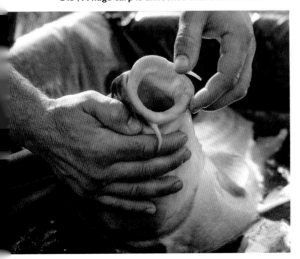

246 | Fishing in Paris is a cultural experience too

248 | **An experienced carper's setup at Etang le Fays**

247
One of the French greats
Les Quis, France
Spring to end of fall
Carp

In France, carp fishing took off around twenty years ago and has revolutionized this branch of the sport. Les Quis was one of the pioneering complexes and is still considered one of the best. Its four lakes all produce carp weighing up to 60 lb (27 kg) and more and the setting is tranquil and unspoiled. The carp are here in numbers and all you have to do is catch them. This is an adventure for sure, but an extremely comfortable one at that.

248
The latest thing
Etang Le Fays, Champagne-Ardennes, France
All year
Carp

This is one of the most famous of the modern-style carp-fisheries that have sprung up in France. It is also up there with the best. With seventeen glorious acres (7 hectares) this really is a haven. There are carp well over 60 lb (27 kg) and there is even a little pond full of smaller carp for children, or just a bit of fun. A welcoming lodge and great food complete the package. Expect more action in the warmer months.

249
Carp classic
Lake of Saint-Cassien, Côte d'Azur, France
April to September
Carp

Cassien is the lake that staggered the carp-fishing world forty years ago. Anglers discovered the 2.3 sq mi (6 sq km) of carp paradise and the sport has never been the same since. The lake is split into three distinct arms with mouth-watering bays, plateaus, weed beds, gravels, rocky outcrops, and submerged islands. Carp of massive proportions still exist here and Cassien remains one of the great angling challenges.

This massive common is lovingly cradled by one of a worldwide army of carp addicts

250
BUCKET LIST FISH: Carp
LAC DE VILLEDON, FRANCE

In many European countries, carp are arguably the most popular rod-caught species of fish and have been responsible for tackle- and bait-revolutions. And it is easy to see why. Carp are big, in excess of 60 lb (27 kg), beautiful, hard-fighting, and extremely difficult to outwit. The smaller crucian carp has become a cult quarry for many traditional anglers too. The common carp, and its varieties the mirror and the leather carp, thrive throughout North America, most of Eurasia, Australia, as well as in pockets of South Africa and India.

251
All the seas can offer
Mediterranean coast, Toulon, France
April to May, August to mid-November
Pelagic species

There are some tremendous fly-fishing adventures along the French Mediterranean coast. Target fish are the pelagics—mackerel, skipjack tuna, and striped bonito. The key is to keep mobile and explore, either by wading or preferably by kayak. You need to be able to get big flies out far and fast, so double hauling is a useful skill. This is not an easy challenge but the first run of a wild bonito is an experience you'll never forget.

252
High-altitude trout
Massif Central rivers, France
Spring to fall
Trout

Oh to spend a few days exploring the wild rivers of the Massif Central in the south of France. The upper Dordogne is the best known, but the area is riddled with streams and tributaries like the Maronne, Doustre, and La Bave. In these small, crystal-clear environments a single poor cast can spell disaster. The fly-angler can travel light, keep mobile, and run into schools of grayling. There are also black bass in the nearby lakes.

253
Schools of gold
Lot River, southern France
Summer
Barbel, carp

The Lot River flows for 300 mi (483 km) through southern France and is well-known for its large carp weighing 70 lb (32 kg) or more. However, in the quicker, shallower reaches upstream of the town of Cahors, barbel are prolific, hard-fighting, and a joy to catch in crystal-clear water. The average size is only around 4 lb (1.8 kg) but you can stalk bigger, individual fish with sweetcorn and float gear. Enjoy fishing in some of Europe's most breathtaking countryside.

254
A French legend
Paradise Lake, Limoges, France
All year
Carp

Paradise is regarded as one of the top carp waters in France and has earned a huge reputation over the years. It's another attractive, secluded water surrounded by tree-clad hills. Carp of 60 lb (27 kg) are not uncommon and, when conditions are right, multiple hook-ups can be achieved. The lake has a good cold-weather history, food is available on site, and the advice has a great reputation. Even airport pick-ups are offered at a reasonable price.

251 | **The sea shimmers with Mediterranean mackerel**

Catfish can grow to massive sizes. This is a big one but there are bigger ones out there!

255
BUCKET LIST FISH: Freshwater catfish
FRANCE

There are many catfish species, but the one that interests anglers the most is the wels—the giant that is native to central and Eastern Europe and has been introduced into Western Europe and colonized most of France's major rivers. Weights have been recorded of up to 700 lb (320 kg) or more and hundred pounders (45 kg) are common. The catfish's extreme size is matched by ferocious fighting abilities, and exhilarating battles can last for hours. Lures can work, but dead baits are preferred; everything from dead frogs to chicken entrails have been used to catch these fish.

256
An experience magnifique
Loire River, Tours, France
Summer
Catfish and barbel

If you base yourself close to Tours, there is some great fishing for gigantic "cats" in the Loire and thoroughly engaging opportunities for barbel. The barbel might not be massive but it can be plentiful and sight-fishing is often possible, especially in stunning tributaries like the Indre and the Cher. Fishing for the catfish is more static but summer is a great time to stalk barbel, chub, and perch in the bright water. This is just about the perfect angling adventure in this historic area of France.

257
Rivers of big cats
French Rivers, France
Spring to fall
Catfish

"Cats" are not indigenous to France but they have been resident for many years and have become a major part of the fishing scene. Many of the carp lakes hold big "cats," but if it is adventure you seek, then the rivers are a must. The Seine and the Gironde are notables but some of the most memorable fishing is on the Loire, the Lot, and the Tarn. There will be exploring to do and a boat helps, but if it is enormous fish you are after in glorious settings then look no farther.

257 | **French catfishing takes many anglers to the River Tarn**

258
Colossal catfish
Ebro River, Catalonia, Spain
Summer and fall
Wels catfish

Wels catfish . . . whether you love them or loathe them, there is no disputing they grow huge; well over 250 lb (113 kg) in the lower Ebro, south of Barcelona. The battle with these fish is unforgettable. You can expect long runs of line and anything up to an hour of struggle with a fish bigger than you are. You can bait-fish but lure-fishing in quick water is the ultimate; it's like hooking a tornado. Much of the river runs through nature reserves so you can expect to see booted and short-toed eagles, peregrine falcons, and black kites.

259
Trout in forgotten waters
Arazas River, Ordesa y Monte Perdido National Park, Spain
March to November
Brown and zebra trout

If pristine trout in ice-clean rivers running beneath towering mountains are your thing, then the Arazas is a river you simply must explore. The rivers flow beneath snow-capped mountains and through forests which are home to bear and wild hog. Stocks of wild brown trout remain high, along with an ancient strain of zebra trout: recognizable by its black and red spotting and four dark stripes down its flanks. This is demanding, wild fishing in a forgotten region of Europe.

258 | **The mighty Ebro river**

The brown trout offers numerous shapes and colors and is perhaps the most widely spread fish species on the planet

260
BUCKET LIST FISH: Brown trout (sea trout)
SPAIN

This gloriously beautiful strain of trout could well be the sportfisher's favorite target. Since its spread around the world from the late nineteenth century, it has reached pretty much every continent. "Browns" can be caught everywhere from mountain streams to deep reservoirs. Sometimes different strains run to sea, or turn from an invertebrate diet to one of small fish; either way it can grow huge. The colossal variety in looks, lifestyles, habitats, and sizes ensures no angler can ever tire of these wonderful fish. For the world fly-angler, a pristine, wild "brownie" has to be the ultimate prize.

261 | **Early morning at Ullíbarri-Gamboa reservoir**

262 | **A black bass attempts to throw the hook**

261
Spain's unknown monsters
Central and northern Spain
March to April, June to July, and September to early October
Brown trout

If you are looking for a mega, pioneering adventure, this could be it. The story begins with the vast reservoirs built years ago to provide Spain with its water supply. From the dams of these reservoirs, there often run wide, deep, crystal-clear, oxygen-rich, and chillingly cold rivers. These are the perfect habitats for brown trout, growing huge on small fish and shrimp. Fish of trophy size are there to be caught if you can find and outwit them. There are also reports of self-sustaining populations of huchen, brought over from Eastern European rivers and now flourishing in Spain. This is mouth-watering stuff for any fly fisher.

262
Mega pike and bass
Cíjara Reservoir, Extremadura/Castilla la Mancha, Spain
All year, but best April and September
Northern pike, largemouth black bass

In Extremadura, there are a number of absolutely huge lakes, which hold some of the biggest carp in Europe, but some of these lakes also hold some of the biggest pike in the world. The Cíjara is a vast reservoir, created by damming up the mighty Guadiana River, and it sits in breathtaking Mediterranean landscapes. In spring, the pike are easiest to find in shallower water near the many small islands, and in fall the big pike are mostly found in open water, and caught on jigs. Cíjara is also extremely popular with bass anglers; many very big bass are caught here.

263 | Lake Zahara has a lunar beauty all of its own

264 | Opulent fishing at Puerto Banus in Marbella

263
A jewel set in the mountains of Spain

Lake Zahara, Ronda, Spain
May to September
Black bass

Zahara is a large, remote reservoir in the mountains of the Sierra de Grazalema. Fishing from the shore is possible here and very large black bass are found in bays, inlets, and under any marginal structures. The water is generally clear so fish can be sighted. Keep on the move and work lures, poppers, and big flies close to any features. Early morning and evenings are best and it is wise to avoid the heat of midday. Take a break; visit the historic, fortified town that looks over the water, and enjoy a glass of something refreshing in the pretty plaza.

264
Sun, sangria, and smashing sea bass

Marbella Coast, Spain
Spring to fall
Sea bass

When you think of fishing around Marbella, the star attraction is charter work for tuna and swordfish on a boat out of Puerto Banus. This can be fantastic if you have the time and the money, however, the beaches around the town offer great bass potential both for fly and lure fishing. Location is important, so look for gulls working over prey fish and also the many inlets where streams and rivers enter the sea. Timing is critical: early morning can see bass coming in very close and the beaches are deserted until 10:00 a.m. or so. Get your fishing done early, then enjoy the day.

265

The golden barbel of the south

Guadiaro River, Cádiz Province, Spain

March to October, but check local spawning restrictions

Andalusian barbel

This river is a hidden gem, all 100 mi (161 km) of it. It coils through mountains, wildflower meadows, olive groves, and the traditional white villages of southern Spain. It is a shallow, crystal-clear river with dancing shallows and deeper, mysterious pools. The barbel are a colorful strain with canary yellow bellies, averaging 3 or 4 lb (1.4 to 1.8 kg). There are plenty of them, but best of all they can easily be fly-caught. Yes, you can even take them off the surface with tiny black dries. Nowhere else can you do this . . . or see so many golden orioles as you fish.

266

Bonito bonito

Gibraltar Bay, Gibraltar

October to February

Atlantic bonito

At the mouth of Gibraltar Bay, many different types of prey gather through the course of a year; from swimming crab, to flying fish. The bonito comes in winter to hunt small horse mackerel. The most effective method for catching them is free-lining a small, live mackerel in a circle-hook on the surface. The bonito are, like other mackerel types, very hard fighters, and when you get them on standard tackle they give you long runs for their size. It's a lot of fun. The bonito at Gibraltar usually range from 4.5 to 11 lb (2 to 5 kg), occasionally with fish between 15 and 20 lb (6.8 and 9 kg). The maximum size is about 24 lb (11 kg).

267
Giants of the two seas
The Straits of Gibraltar, Gibraltar
Spring to fall
Tuna, grouper, swordfish, marlin

This is all about deep-sea drama at the pinch point between the Atlantic Ocean and the Mediterranean Sea. Fish of many species travel from one water body to another and the Straits offer the ideal ambush point. This is a venue beset by the winds, the tides, and violent currents as the cold of the Atlantic meets the warmth of the Mediterranean. Add the topography of underwater mountains, canyons, and reefs, as well as heavy commercial boat-traffic, and you'll see why an experienced skipper is a must.

268
Deep-sea scrapper
The Straits of Gibraltar, Gibraltar
Summer
Dentex bream

The Straits of Gibraltar are a fascinating mix of currents, tides, and wind patterns, along with vast underwater depth changes. This all adds up to perfect territory for predatorial fish, including the feisty dentex bream. These fish seldom exceed 30 lb (13 kg) but they fight with power and doggedness. You can catch them by trolling, drifting with live bait, or jigging down close to rocks and wrecks. In summer, the bream come closer to shore and you can do without the expense of going afloat.

267, 268 | The sun sets over the Straits of Gibraltar

269
Eel and bream on the reef
Coastal reefs, Gibraltar
All year, but conger best April to June
European conger, dentex sea bream

On Gibraltar's Mediterranean coast, there
are some deeper areas with towering reefs.
These reefs are not easy to anchor on
because of the ever-changing currents, but
this is where congers can be found in good
numbers. You can catch congers on pieces
of fish, but they especially love live squid.
Unfortunately—or fortunately, depending
how you look at it—so do the dentex sea
bream. The congers average from 22 to 33 lb
(10 to 15 kg), the dentex from 9 to 15 lb
(4 to 6.8 kg), and both types of fish fight
extremely hard, even on heavy gear.

270
Mini-tarpon sport
Guadiana River, Portugal
April to end of June
Shad

Think of shad as mini tarpon on your line—
they certainly spend as much time airborne.
Shad are in decline in many rivers around
Europe but they still run in the Guadiana in
huge numbers every spring as they come
from the sea to spawn. Most are twaite shad
of 2 to 3 lb (0.9 to 1.4 kg) but every now
and again the larger cousin, the allis shad,
might appear. These can be twice the size
and the fight is even more hairy. Fly-gear
is perfect with a barbless fly. Yes, you'll lose
fish but catch-and-release is easier and these
are fragile fish.

270 | The Guadiana is host to gigantic runs of the scintillating shad

271

A place to explore
Guadiana River, Portugal
Summer and fall
Comizo barbel

Freshwater-fishing in Portugal is all about exploration and therein lies the adventure. There is superb sport to be had with carp, catfish, pike, black bass, and several smaller barbel species but it is the giant Comizo strain that stirs the blood. They grow to 40 lb (18 kg) plus and though you can catch them with carp tactics in the slow, deep pools, using moving baits in rapid water is electric sport. The Guadiana is a great river to start on but the whole country is riddled with possibilities waiting to be explored.

272

Portuguese peace
Valle de Gaio, Portugal
July to October
Black bass

Bass have done well in the Iberian Peninsula and thrive in the warm weather that the south of Europe enjoys. This enchanting location is a reservoir, as many of the still waters in Portugal and Spain are, but that does not detract from its beauty or the magic of its setting. There are tales of big bass here and the shoreline is indented with many bass-holding territories. Like most bass fishing, best times are early morning and sunset when you conveniently escape the heat of the day.

271 | **The River Guadiana holds huge numbers of Comizo barbel**

272 | **Sunset fishing in Portugal**

273
Hunting the European bonefish
The Algarve, Portugal
May to September
Mullet

Mullet swarm the entire coastline of the Mediterranean and the warmer areas of the Atlantic, even as far north as Scotland on occasion, but the Algarve is a wonderful place to fish for them. Mullet—whether thick-lipped, thin-lipped, or even golden-grays—are tricky to fool on either bait or fly. They are not called the "gray ghosts" for nothing, and the best starting point will be harbors and places where the fish are used to seeing waste-food, most especially bread. Hook one on light gear and just wait for that scorching first run that makes all the frustration worthwhile.

274
Big blues in the amazing Azores
Ponta Delgada, Azores, Portugal
July, August, September
Blue marlin

If you are looking for "blues" of 500 lb (226 kg) and more, the Azores is the place for you. Here, records are broken and skippers are among the most experienced in the world. They all have their favorite grounds and some, like the Condor and Bank Azores, are world famous. There are fish reaching 1,000 lb (454 kg) and others that fight more out of the water than in. High summer is the time to go, then the Azores high-pressure system is generally sitting over this part of the Atlantic and seas are calm. As well as the fishing, there are dolphins to watch and the legendary gardens on shore.

275

A river of endless possibilities

Guadiana River, Mertola, Portugal

April and May for shad

Shad, comizo barbel, zander

The Guadiana is one of Europe's big rivers, much of its length marks the Spanish/Portuguese border. Shad run the river in vast numbers in the spring and can be caught on a fly or with small spinners. The comizos grow huge and are one of the iconic fish of Europe, reaching 30 lb (13 kg) and more. Zander round off this list of mouthwatering opportunities, all of which can be caught in this intriguing river surrounded by natural landscapes and steeped in history, culture, and opportunities for good food.

276

As tough as it gets

Northumbrian Coast, England

Winter

Cod

It's true that the North Sea cod stocks aren't what they were, but England's northeast coast can produce invigorating sport for cod and codling through the winter months. Shore-fishing on wild, stormy nights isn't for everyone, but it can be inspiring and extremely satisfying. Search out the rocky headlands and cliffs, especially those that look over kelp beds. Take into account the tides and winds and their directions, and ensure your baits, generally lug and peeler crabs, are as fresh as you can get them. Amble is a great center. Take all local advice, which might lead you to the legendary Saltpan Rocks where many cod have been taken in the past.

276 | In Northumberland, cod fishing does not get wilder—especially when a northerly wind howls in

The king of fish—the Atlantic salmon—sought over centuries for its size, glamor, and magical lifestyle

277
BUCKET LIST FISH: Atlantic salmon
NORTHEAST ENGLAND AND SCOTLAND

The eggs of the salmon are laid in the headwaters of cold, clean rivers. The young fish make their way to the open seas and spend years there, growing into big, silver fish that return to freshwater to complete their life cycle, spawn, and, usually, die. It is no wonder that these buccaneering fish have come to represent the epitome of sporting challenges. In the past, wherever a river entered the Atlantic, in Canada, America, or Europe, it would likely have a run of these fish. Today, salmon rivers are more rare, protected, and often expensive. The River Spey is the birthplace of the two–handed rod that has become popular for fishing salmon and steelhead on large rivers everywhere.

278
Great accessible salmon sport
Tyne River, northeast England
February/March to October
Atlantic salmon

Not long ago, the Tyne River was devastated by pollution due to its industrial past, but painstaking conservation efforts have turned it into one of the great salmon rivers of Europe. Best of all, access to super fishing in glorious hill country is easy and relatively cheap. Thanks to frequent water releases from Kielder Dam, salmon run the Tyne most weeks of the season and while fly-fishing is encouraged, fish-friendly spinning techniques with a single hook are allowed.

279
Stately-home tenching
Blickling Lake, Norfolk, England
July to October
Tench

Blickling Hall is one of the great houses of England, once home to the Boleyn family of Tudor fame. The house and park make a grand setting for this fabulous 30-acre (12-hectare) tench paradise. Tench feed until around midday, but there are roach and bream to keep sport ticking along. Try a float off the dam in deep water, or fishing from openings in the reeds toward the house itself. And the fabulous beaches of north Norfolk are barely half an hour away.

280
Rich and shallow waters
Broadland, Norfolk Broads, England
November to mid-March
Pike, perch

The Norfolk Broads are sheets of shallow water where the land was dug out for peat—a fuel used centuries ago. These still waters, like Hickling and Horsey, are linked by the mainly tidal Thurne, Yare, Bure, and Ant rivers and become predator-rich once winter sets in. Broadland produces record perch and pike every year. Target still and running water and keep on the move. Don't neglect the riverside towns like Wroxham.

281
Coast shark
Brancaster Bay, Norfolk, England
All year, but tope is best May to September
Tope, Atlantic mackerel, European sea bass

This area is prone to significant tidal changes and strong currents. Besides the private boats, numerous charter boats offer trips with all gear included. Target fish are tope, spurdog shark, skate, sea bass, and mackerel. A good way to catch the tope is by anchoring up, chumming with mackerel offal, and hooking a piece of mackerel on a big single hook behind a sand-grip lead.

283 | Thames Weir Pools are the stuff of angling dreams, home to mighty perch, pike, and barbel

282

The cradle of fly-fishing
Test River, southern England
Best April to September
Brown trout

The crystal-clear waters of the Test are famed worldwide as the cradle of both dry-fly and nymph techniques for brown trout. The peak of the fishing takes place in late May and early June when the glorious mayfly hatch and trout gorge on the golden insects. Most of the beats, especially around the lovely town of Stockbridge, are historically famous and they are all looked after meticulously by expert river keepers. For a price, you can fly-fish in this perfect setting and then take tea in a riverside hut as the meadows glow in the sunset.

283

Weir pool action
Thames Weir Pools, England
June to September
Perch

The Thames is famous for cracking perch, and during the summer they congregate in the many weir pools upriver of London. Top of the list are Goring, Mapledurham, and Pangbourne—all of which are best fished by boat. The water will be deep with swirling currents and it is necessary to get lures and baits down deep with control. Early mornings are best, before the world wakes, when the Thames Valley is a wonderland of mists where you can still sense the world of Ratty and Mole from Kenneth Grahame's novel *The Wind In The Willows*.

284
Best bet for a forty
Chew Valley Lake, Bristol, England
February, October, and November
Pike

Can you imagine catching a 40 lb (18 kg) pike on the fly? Well it has been done, on Chew Valley Lake, a 1.9 sq mi (4.8 sq km) reservoir in the southwest of England. For a reservoir, Chew is relatively shallow, very fertile, and full of both prey-fish and stocked-trout. Pike-fishing is limited to three months of the year, leaving these monsters to thrive on food and a lack of angling pressure. Fish from either the bank or a boat, with dead bait or lure, and you have no better chance of a fabled "thirty" anywhere in the world. The surrounding Mendip Hills provide the perfect backdrop to the trophy shot of your life.

285
Classic river, classic species
Avon River, Hampshire, England
December to mid-March
Roach

The roach has been the UK's favorite species for generations and the Hampshire Avon is its most iconic home. Fisheries like Britford, Longford, Ringwood, and the Royalty are legendary for fish of 2 and even 3 lb (0.9 to 1.4 kg), especially now the roach numbers are returning after a period of drought. Winter is the hot time when the wet westerlies blow and the river is carrying some color. Trotting with a centerpin and stick-float is the acknowledged method, and bread or maggots the bait. These might not be massive fish but they are regarded as the ultimate river angler's challenge.

285 | The mighty River Avon is legendary for its roach and fly-fishing

286
Giant ladies of the stream
Frome River, Dorset, England
November to March
Grayling

The Frome is excellent for trout but it is the stock of grayling that makes it globally renowned. It's a small river that winds through countryside and the valley remains largely unspoiled in its upper reaches. Winter nymph fishing in the clear waters is superb and over 3 lb (1.4 kg) grayling are always a possibility, even a probability if you are fortunate. The UK record fell here a few years back at 4.5 lb (2 kg) and sightings of even larger fish have been reported.

287
Predator paradise
Lower Severn River, England
Summer to fall
Zander

Zander are hard to catch, require dedication, and, realistically, the Lower Severn is their stronghold in the UK. A boat is an advantage as the schools group up around snags and underwater features far from accessible banks. You can bait fish but the experts always go for lures, little jig heads especially, and this will keep you mobile and engaged. Try to get out at dawn—the best time for fishing, and to appreciate the glorious setting.

288
Self-sustaining beauties
Wye River, Buxton, England
April to September (trout), November to end of February (grayling)
Wild rainbow trout, grayling

One reason fishing here is special is that this is the only UK river where rainbows breed naturally. Pursuing these unique fish is about stealth and putting a fly (generally a dry) to a fish you have sighted. Add on a visit to the Wye's sister rivers, the Derwent, Lathkill, and Dove, where author and angler Izaak Walton's collaborator, Charles Cotton, had his fishing hut; it still exists after 300 years.

289
Cast into the carp record book
Redmire Pool, Herefordshire, England
Mid-June to late October
Carp

Redmire is well-known by those who love carp fishing for the record-breaking specimens found there over the last century. For seventy years it has had reserved access but now, for a price, fishing this hallowed venue is open to a lucky few. The 3-acre (1.2-hectare) lake nestles in a private estate and is a haven of peace and tranquility—and big carp. Whether the monsters of old still exist is a question for you to find out.

290

Shark ahoy!

Cornish coast, England
April and May
Porbeagle shark

The rugged north Cornish coast is the place to go for these true big-game fish that can still be caught on 30 lb (13 kg) class tackle. These are large, hard-fighting sharks but you needn't go in over-gunned and the fight can be a raw, personal duel between angler and fish. They like to hang relatively close to the shore and and most are caught 1 mi (1.6 km) or so out, generally on mackerel baits presented under a float. It's a great experience within hailing distance of this enchanting, cliff-strewn coastline. A hidden gem.

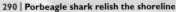

290 | **Porbeagle shark relish the shoreline**

291
A magic valley
Wye River, border of England and Wales
June to October
Barbel

The Wye provides barbel-fishing at its
European best. The shallows allow you to
bounce baits like worms and meat while the
uninterrupted glides encourage float-fishing.
Deep mysterious pools are perfect for more
static ledgering techniques, so the variety is
staggering. The Wye wends through superb
countryside from the north in Wales through
historic English towns like Ross in the south.
Ancient churches, ruined castles, mountains,
and forests all provide the perfect barbel-
fisher's backdrop.

292
Rugged rocks, splendid bass
Monkstone Point, Pembrokeshire Coast, Wales
Summer and fall
Sea bass

Pembrokeshire offers some of the best, most
accessible, wild shore-fishing in Europe and
in addition to Monkstone Point, there are
many other places to explore in this
magnificent, unspoiled landscape. Look for
rocky headlands, boulders, weed-beds, sandy
areas, reefs, channels, and tidal rips where
bass love to feed. Take a variety of lures with
differing actions, colors, and weights, or if
you prefer bait, peeler crabs and sand eels
are impossible to beat. But watch out for the
quick tides, and never risk being stranded.

291 | **The Wye was famous for salmon but now it is a top barbel river**

An angler with a sea bass caught off the Welsh coast

293

BUCKET LIST FISH: European sea bass

PEMBROKESHIRE COAST, UK

There are many examples of marine bass worldwide, but the two true icons are the European sea bass and the North American "striper"—striped sea bass. The former has a range from southern Norway to the Black Sea, grows well into double figures weight-wise (over 11 lb; 5 kg), and is beloved by shore lure- and fly-anglers. Fishing the surf for these silver warriors is a fabulous experience. The striped bass is found along the Atlantic and Gulf coasts of North America and can grow to a staggering 100 lb (45 kg) or more, so it's hardly a surprise that it, too, has legions of obsessive followers. Hooking a big striper, in a big surf, is a big memory for life.

Loch Garry

White-tailed sea eagle fishing

Catch and release trout

294

Loch of leopard-spotted trout

Loch Garry, Inverness-shire, Scotland

April to late September

Ferox trout

Ferox are large, cannibalistic brown trout that live in glacial lochs of Europe and represent one of today's great angling challenges. Loch Garry is a remote, high-altitude loch (lake) of staggering natural beauty that has produced huge fish in the recent past, generally through trolling techniques. However, fly-fishing for these monsters is a genuine possibility if you can get afloat. Target these extraordinary fish in high summer at dusk and dawn when they feed on char in the surface layers. Watch out for eagles and red deer on the shoreline.

295
Silver beauties of the tides
North Uist, Hebrides, Scotland
April to October
Sea trout

Sea and golden eagles in the sky; dolphins and seals around the coast; an island that is more water than land, forever washed by the tides that bring seemingly limitless runs of sea trout into the pools; North Uist is a remote island, glorious in its solitude, a venue where the angler feels truly alone with some of the most hard-fighting fish in Europe. Locations on the island like Vallay, Dusary, and Horisary are historic places and when the tide turns and the schools surge in from the sea, fry and shrimp patterned-flies are hit with unbelievable ferocity.

296
The Scottish classic
Tay River, central Scotland
Spring to fall
Atlantic salmon

One of Scotland's "classic" salmon rivers, the Tay is generally shallow with miles of broken water, perfect for the fly angler. Fall runs of big fish are especially famous as are the freshwater pearl oysters that have made the Tay one of their last refuges. Celebrated tributaries like the River Isla hold huge grayling and also big numbers of recently, and controversially, introduced beavers. For the malt whisky connoisseurs, the Tay valley offers countless after-fishing tipples.

295 | **North Uist is a spellbinding destination**

296 | **Releasing an Atlantic salmon**

298 | Fishing boats are put to no better use than on Lough Melvin

297
Stunning shore action
Jersey, Channel Islands
March to November
Sea bass

Jersey has incredible tidal ranges, clear water, and is riddled with bass-holding locations and features. Every beach, inlet, reef, rocky outcrop, gully, harbor, weed-bed, and tidal rip screams to be fished for these silver buccaneers of the sea. For the lure-angler this is bass heaven and you could fish every mark on the island for years and never exhaust its possibilities. All this choice means that fishing pressure is light and bass come to lures with unsuspecting ferocity. Don't forget your chest waders so you can get into the shallows and fully explore this amazing island.

298
Trout of rainbow colors
Lough Melvin, border of Ireland and Northern Ireland
April to end of September
Salmon, char, and four species of trout

Beautiful Lough Melvin is 7 mi (11 km) long, 2 mi (3 km) wide, nearly 150 ft (46 m) deep, and a natural history phenomenon. From its waters you can, at times, catch salmon, brown trout, ferox trout, sonaghan trout, and gillaroo trout. This variety makes it unique, and it is the last two species of trout that make the lough especially revered. The sonaghan are silver-colored, slim, and fight like banshees. The gillaroo are snail-feeders and dramatically spotted in splashes of black and gold. Four trout sub-species in a day? Now there's a challenge.

299
Fish like battleships
Ireland
July to early November
Bluefin tuna

The return of the awe-inspiring bluefin tuna
to the waters of Britain and Ireland is one
of the great marine conservation success
stories. A limited number of skippers have
licenses to fish for these giants out of ports
like Galway, Donegal, Sligo, and Kinsale.
Watching these giant fish slicing into the
schools of mackerel is a dawn-of-time
experience and the ensuing fight is back-
breaking. All fish are tagged, and often
DNA samples are taken before they are
painstakingly released. It's a truly life-
changing experience.

300
River of monsters
River Shannon, Ireland
February to September
Atlantic salmon

For decades, the Shannon has been one of
the worldwide locations for enormous fish,
and even though its best days might be over,
this is still a river of dreams. Castleconnell
fishery was an iconic name in the past, with
limitless fish caught in excess of 40 lb
(18 kg), and to this day it produces big, early-
season fish. There are good grilse runs from
May to the end of June along the eight beats
here, each around half a mile (800 m) long.
The Shannon is a big, powerful river here
and a 14 ft (4.2 m) double-handed rod can
be an advantage, and there are runs where
careful wading gives the edge.

300 | The surf on Ireland's west coast is a fisher's paradise

301

Taking it easy in the heart of Ireland

River Shannon, Ireland
June to October
Tench, bream, rudd

At 224 mi (360 km) from source to sea, the Shannon is the longest river in the British Isles and one of the most beautiful. Take a cruiser for this adventure and you will be able to fish more of the river and reach unending loughs and backwaters which a bank-bound angler could not access. Where you start and where you finish is a tough one but centers such as Carrick-on-Shannon and Lanesborough offer great sport, especially bream. Rudd and tench are always exciting possibilities and from a boat you can bait quiet areas and go back to them each evening for the best of the sport.

302

Heavy fish, light gear

Atlantic coast, Ireland
May to September (but winter for the biggest fish)
Pollock

The West Coast of Ireland is an angler's wonderland of harbors, headlands, piers, reefs, kelp-beds, and rocks—all features that scream pollock. This is true pollock paradise and that means white-knuckle sport with fish in 13 to 19 lb (6 to 8.5 kg) range. The way to go is fishing light with lures of all sorts, especially rubbers. You can even go on the fly with arm-aching results. Keep mobile, which can call for agility, or perhaps going afloat in a kayak. This is wild fishing for wild fish in a wild terrain.

302 | The loveliness and loneliness of the Irish west coast

304 | **Lough Corrib mayfly hatches are thick as snowstorms, the air white with dancing flies—huge trout result**

303
Great days for mighty rays
The Shannon Estuary, Ireland
May to October
Thornback ray

There's something very special about this experience because you are catching these sporting sea-fish as far as 30 mi (48 km) up a river estuary. The Shannon is in itself a fishing phenomenon, perhaps the great river of Europe, and in its lower reaches it is paved with these hard-fighting rays. Mackerel are the best bait and in the sheltered waters you can fish with comparatively light gear which only increases the sport. As an added bonus, bull huss are also frequently caught in this compelling Irish world of water.

304
Where mayfly explode
Lough Corrib, north of Galway, Ireland
April to late September
Brown trout

Corrib is 33 mi (53 km) long, dotted with 365 islands and full of pristine brown trout. However, it is the mayfly season between mid-May and early June that makes Corrib extraordinary. This is when the biggest trout come to the surface to gorge on them, and dapping is the method. A 15 ft (4.5 m) rod, a silk or floss line, a length of nylon, and a hook is all you need. You bait with two mayfly and let the breeze catch the floss line so that they dance on the surface before your boat. Watch for the nose of a monster coming to engulf them. This is an ancient skill, easily mastered, and as thrilling as fishing can get.

305
Huge fish, huge waters

The Western Loughs of Conn, Mask, and
Corrib, Connemara, Ireland
April to early December
Pike

For 200 years, the vast western loughs have
been famed for monster pike, and here you
are fishing in the mists of history. Enormous
pike still exist, growing large on a diet of
trout, salmon, and coarse fish. The mobility
of lure fishing produces numbers of pike
but often the biggest come to a more static
dead-bait approach. The scenery is wild and
wonderful, but as you'll be boat fishing
beware of violent changes in the weather. It
is no hardship to pull off early, as the "craic"
in the Guinness-rich pubs is another local
specialty to be savored.

306
A wild west-coast experience

Kerry Coast, Ireland
June to November
Bass, pollock, wrasse

The Kerry Coast has been a bass delight
since the 1960s, and for good reason. This is
a spectacular coastline framed by mountains
and laced with bass-holding features. It is a
paradise for the lure angler and it's wise to
take the whole selection of Rapalas, plastics,
and heavy spoons to achieve big distances.
Chest-waders are essential and it helps if you
have a degree of agility to get you to the best
spots. The weather is unpredictable and if
bass are a long shot there is terrific sport for
pollock and wrasse. Waterville is a top center
for the exploring angler, and a guide here
can prove their worth.

305 | **The great Irish loughs offer phenomenal fishing**

306 | **Find shore species like pollock on the Kerry Coast**

307

Yards of silver

Lough Currane, County Kerry, Ireland

April to September

Sea trout

Currane is Ireland's premier sea-trout
location and attracts an international
following—even the legendary Charlie
Chaplin loved the Lough like no other.
It's a huge water, 4 sq mi (10 sq km), and
can get battered by westerly winds coming
in from the Atlantic. Top sea-trout locations
with names like Black Point and Rough
Island suggest this is not fishing for the
faint-hearted but the Lough boasts some
of the best guides in Europe. Sport can
be hectic with sea trout running into
double figures along with a high chance
of salmon and grilse.

308

Outstanding salmon river

River Blackwater at Cork, County
Waterford, Ireland

Open season February to September

Atlantic salmon

The Cork Blackwater is world renowned
and Ireland's finest salmon river. Lovely,
green, rolling hills, tree-lined shores,
a good steady flow, and salmon runs all
through the season, make this river an
angler's dream. The salmon vary from
2 to 20 lb (0.9 to 9 kg), with the biggest
entering the river in the fall. The main
baits are flies on sink-tip lines, but many
fish are also caught on lures, spoons,
Devon spinners, and on preserved, dyed
shrimp under a drifting float.

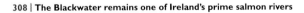

308 | The Blackwater remains one of Ireland's prime salmon rivers

AFRICA AND THE MIDDLE EAST

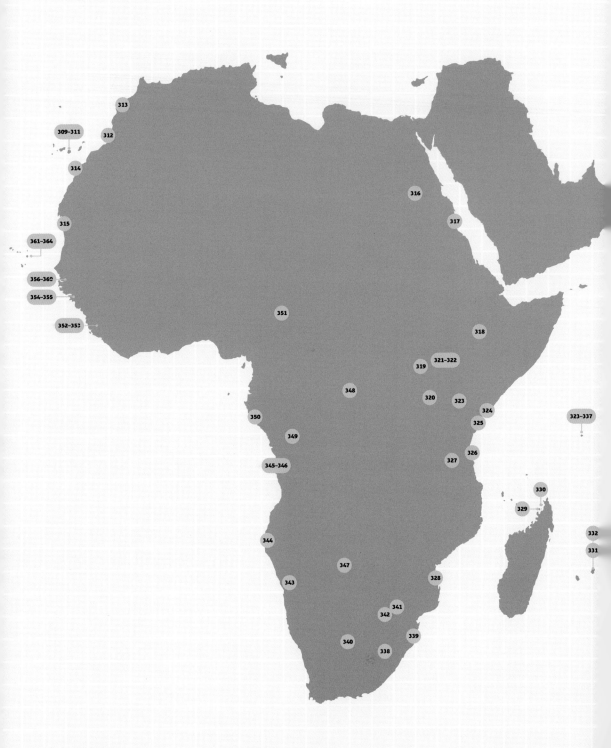

AFRICA AND THE MIDDLE EAST: ENTRY LIST

310 | The bigeye tuna lives up to its name and Gran Canaria is a great destination for it

309
Marlin on Europe's doorstep
Pasito Blanco, Gran Canaria
May to October
Blue marlin, white marlin

This classic Spanish marina has berths for 388 craft up to a maximum length of 131 ft (40 m)—so no super yachts, but plenty of sailboats, motorboats, and other vessels count this harbor as home and offer a wide choice when it comes to picking a charter to take you out into the Atlantic in search of blue or white marlin. The season starts in May, and Gran Canaria's relative proximity to Europe makes it a popular destination for sportfishing. Trolling is still the favored method here, and charters are happy to tailor trips for experienced anglers and novices alike.

310
All night long for bigeye tuna
Puerto Base, Gran Canaria
March to April
Bigeye tuna

Plumper than the yellowfin and—as its name suggests—with larger eyes, the bigeye is a fast-growing fish that can measure over 5 ft (1.5 m) in length and weigh up to 400 lb (181 kg). The best time to fish for bigeyes is usually dawn and dusk, but a good skipper will be able to advise you about any local variations—sometimes, for example, it's possible to troll all night when it's a full moon, and if there's fog laying on the water you can catch them, on and off, all day.

311
Scrapping with "reef donkeys"
Puerto Rico, Gran Canaria
October to April
Amberjack

Nicknamed "reef donkeys"—probably as a
nod to their somewhat homely appearance
and legendary stubbornness—amberjacks
have a deserved reputation as hard-fighting
fish that are tough to land and terrific fun
on light tackle. Amberjacks are drawn to
structures, so seek them out over wrecks or
in and around reefs, and spin or jig for them
with bright metal lures, or use pieces of
mullet, herring, or sardines. Puerto Rico
itself is a lively, bustling port with plenty to
do—and because it's on the south of the
island, it's warmer here for longer.

312
A starkly beautiful bass experience
Ahl Souss Dam, Agadir, Morocco
Spring to fall
African black bass

There are several dams in the sparsely
populated Souss Massa region, in and
around Tamri National Park. Although
many of the lakes hold bass, Ahl Souss is,
perhaps, the anglers' favorite. It's a large
water and is best attacked by kayak or
float-tube. Shore-fishing is possible, but
it is rugged going in the heat. All the usual
bass approaches work and a local guide
is invaluable, both to help with locations
and procuring fishing authorization.
Conservation is rightly revered here and
all bass must be returned immediately.

311 | Puerto Rico is the perfect base to tangle with amberjack

313
A serene carp experience
Lake Bin El Ouidane, near Casablanca, Morocco
Spring to fall
Carp

Bin El Ouidane is a huge, 15,000-acre (6,070-ha) water-storage lake created by a dam built across the El Abid River in the 1950s and stocked with carp in the 1990s. They have grown well and the mirror carp have reached 70 lb (32 kg) with the more dominant common carp not far behind. This a near-unique carp experience. You are fishing in a lunar landscape with mountains, sometimes snow-capped, on the horizon. The lake is remote and, with no light pollution, anglers report extraordinary night skies.

314
Sea bass—the unknown frontier
Moroccan coast, Morocco
April to November
Sea bass

The Moroccan Atlantic coast is well over 1,240 mi (2,000 km) long and much of this remains relatively unexplored by serious anglers. However, around Agadir to the south there is wondrous rock-fishing with amazing surf- and tidal-rips. Rumors of colossal 20 lb (9 kg) plus bass abound, and the locals suggest spring and fall see the best of the fishing. Lure-fishing is generally practiced but fly-fishing opportunities are good, too, as the fish come in close. An amazing experience with lovely people, ancient cultures, and wild fishing in sight of the Sahara desert.

313 | Lake Bin El Ouidane is a stunning location for carp

314 | Fantastic fishing on the Moroccan coast

315
Greyhounds of the sea
Atlantic Coast, Dakhla, Morocco
All year
Leer fish

Is there a faster accelerating sea-target than the leer fish? These torpedoes can grow to 66 lb (30 kg) and their power is simply awesome. The coastline in the region of the Dakhla River mouth is a good place to start your search. Water is deep close in and the key is to fish either the ebb or the flood tide—or both. Leer fish like the fastest currents where they hunt for mullet, sardines, squid, and cuttlefish. You can fish by fly or lure (bait-fish, too) and top-water approaches produce the biggest thrills.

316
Lake of record dreams
Lake Nasser, Aswan, Egypt
Mid-March to mid-May
Nile perch

Nasser is where fishing for huge Nile perch really came to the fore in world sportfishing over thirty years ago. This 300 mi (483 km) long dam, that is central to the economy of Egypt, has produced countless 200 to 300 lb (91 to 136 kg) fish over the decades and still holds monsters. In winter, the perch lurk deep down and trolling is the method, but come spring, the prey-fish swarm in the shallows and that is when fly-fishing comes into its own. Nasser is a breathtaking place, unearthly quiet, with a star-filled sky at night. Bedouin camel-herders might be seen and you are close to all the wonders of ancient Egypt.

316 | **The wonders of the Nile and the desert make fishing here an adventure**

317

Trigger-happy fishing on the flats

Nubian Flats, Port Sudan, Sudan

March to June

Triggerfish, giant trevally

Behind the Nubian Flats is the Nubian desert, in front the Red Sea, and to either side around 400 mi (644 km) of virtually untouched coastline, waiting for the visiting angler to explore. These flats are said to offer the finest triggerfish-angling anywhere in the world and there are still plenty of areas that have never seen an angler or an angler's fly. The landscape may be desolate, but the aquatic environment is superb, and the water so shallow in places that you'll be able to see the tail of the trigger moving proud of the surface as it hones in on a fly.

317 | The Nubian Flats offer absorbing fishing in crystal waters

318 | Trout fishing in Ethiopia is as beautiful and enchanting as it sounds

318
Ethiopa's trout-fishing heaven
Bale Mountains, Ethiopia
December to March and September to October
Trout

Trout-fishing in Ethiopia may sound as unlikely as salmon-fishing in Yemen, and yet the Bale Mountains National Park offers rainbow- and trout-fishing in the Webb, Denko, and Tegona rivers, in a landscape that's more reminiscent of Scotland than the horn of Africa. These fish are the descendants of an enthusiastic stocking program that took place in the 1960s, and they are thriving. Expect deep pools, fast shallow runs, and waterfalls—in fact, there is every kind of feature to enchant the visiting fly-angler. And if you're wondering about the sound, it's probably wild baboons cavorting on the other side of the river.

319
Fishing the Devil's Cauldron
Murchison Falls, Nile River, Uganda
June to August and December to February
Nile perch

Murchison Falls used to be thought of as a venue to be feared and treated with the utmost caution. It is still remote (six hours by road from Entebbe), but landing strips now allow planes in and the experience is far more civilized. The Falls are part of a national park and there are even luxury lodges available. But the fishing is still hair-raising. The so-called Devil's Cauldron is not for the timid. Massive fish fight to the end, and crocs and hippos have an eye open for any unwary anglers. This is all about lure-fishing so refit all your lures with hooks and split-rings that are up for a far tougher job than the manufacturer envisioned.

320
An accessible adventure
Lake Victoria, Uganda
All year, avoid April and May
Nile perch

Victoria is the second biggest water body in the world and has held huge Nile perch since they were stocked here around sixty years ago. The size of the lake can make finding a location difficult but hotspots historically have included Ngamba, Bulago, and Kalangala Island. Trolling is the traditional method for bigger fish and there are several operators who can make fishing accessible and relatively easy. Half- and full-day excursions are offered, making this a relatively untaxing opportunity.

321
The cradle of mankind
Lake Turkana, Kenyan Rift Valley, Kenya
Spring
Nile perch

This is a serious adventure. Turkana is the world's largest permanent desert-lake at 186 mi (300 km) long, 31 mi (50 km) wide, and 328 ft (100 m) deep. It is remote and, in recent years, barely ever fished. Early overland expeditions were successful and big fish exist there today, despite there being more emphasis on local-fishing ventures. A boat will be necessary—the shore is busy with crocodiles—and some of the best fishing is around a large central island.

320 | Lake Victoria is vast but a good guide can put you on to some great fishing

The Nile perch is not only a monster among freshwater species but its silver-sheened flanks are stunning

322
BUCKET LIST FISH: Nile perch
LAKE TURKANA, KENYA

The colossal Nile perch easily exceeds 200 lb (90 kg) and lives in the African rivers, the Nile and the Congo, and many of the continent's great lakes such as Lake Victoria, Lake Turkana, and Lake Nasser. It is a close relative to the Barramundi and, like its saltwater relation, is a tremendous sporting fish. Lake Nasser has long been the most prolific location but venues like Murchison Falls on the Nile itself are perhaps the most dramatic. This awesome predator takes big lures and can be fly-caught but never underestimate this turbo-charged machine of a fish that can strip great lengths of line and then heave itself airborne.

Look for the vivid markings of the brown trout

Elephants drinking at dusk

The Aberdare Mountains cradle some of the most exhilarating trout streams on the planet

323
Lush forests and sparkling streams
Aberdare Mountains, Kenya
June to October
Brown trout

The Aberdare Mountains in Kenya provide a setting that defies all expectations of trout-fishing in Africa. Many of the smaller streams here are fast-flowing, with clear water, narrow crossings, high banks, and lush foliage. There are brownies a-plenty in these streams, many of which have never seen an angler's fly or sensed the tread of waders on the stream-bed, so a sense of adventure is a prerequisite. It's also a good idea to keep an eye on the forest as well as the stream, as animals will often come down to the water to drink.

324

"It's fly-fishing Jim, but not as we know it . . ."

Manda Bay, Lamu archipelago, Kenya
October to November
Sailfish

Visit Manda Bay for fly-fishing with a difference and catch giant sailfish. Here, the flies look more like multi-colored birds than anything resembling an insect, but the sailfish don't care and it's not unusual to catch and release as many as ten fish in a day. All successful sailfishing is a team effort, but while the angler relies as much on the captain and crew as their own skill, there's still something solitary about catching a big sail on a fly—everything around you may descend into organized chaos, but in the eye of the storm, it's just you and the fish.

325

Billfishing at its best

Watamu, Kenya
October to April
Shortbill spearfish

The Watamu Marine Park is the oldest in Africa and is home to coral reefs that provide a rich environment for many sea creatures—especially marine turtles. It's also a luxury resort, perfect for anglers in search of comfort. One of the locations that pioneered the tag-and-release of billfish off the Kenyan coast, Watamu has access to a range of underwater mountains not far offshore, which attract baitfish and their predators, making it perfect for billfish. Shortbills typically grow to between 20 and 60 lb (9 and 27 kg), making them great for first-timers or experienced anglers who like lighter tackle.

324 | **Fly-fishing for Manda Bay sailfish**

326 | **Dogtooth tuna swarm the Arabian Sea**

327 | **Guided tours help anglers to get close to tigerfish**

326
Tuna from the Arabian Sea
Dar es Salaam, Tanzania
**October to December and February
to April**
Dogtooth tuna

Tanzania's largest city is a relative newcomer, having only been established in 1865. It is a rich cultural melting-pot, drawing people from Africa, India, and the Middle East. Its name means "haven of peace" and the port handles about 90 percent of Tanzania's cargo traffic. It's a great place to hire a charter for Latham Island, about 50 nautical miles (93 km) off the coast, which is home to some gigantic dogtooths. Fish the reefs and drop-offs here with lures or live-bait and even if the tuna don't oblige there are plenty of other species—including amberjack, barracuda, and giant trevally—that will.

327
The fast and the furious tigerfish
Ruhudji and Mnyera rivers, Tanzania
August to November
Tigerfish

For many anglers, these two rivers represent the pinnacle in their pursuit of the elusive tigerfish, the toothy predator that averages around 8 lb (3.6 kg) yet fights with a savage determination of a fish twice that size. Imagine if ferocity had fins, and you have the tigerfish. Guided fishing is the way to go, and as water temperatures increase and the water becomes clearer, tigerfish come out to play. The action can be fast and furious, and many an angler has been caught out by that first take, when the tiger hits the fly with the speed of a thief on a motorbike snatching a handbag.

328
Black marlin from blue water
Bazaruto Archipelago, Mozambique
August to April
Black marlin

Catch black marlin against the backdrop of one
of the most stunning landscapes on the planet—
the Bazaruto Archipelago off the coast of
Mozambique. With five islands—four comprised
mainly of sand—no stores, no roads, and home
to a rich ecosphere of marine wildlife (including
what's thought to be the last viable natural
population of dugong in East Africa), this
exquisite archipelago is the jumping-off point
for deep-sea charters that target black marlin,
the largest of the marlin family, and a fish
which can grow to 1,500 lb (680 kg).

328 | **A giant marlin clears
the seas off Mozambique**

329 | **Nosy Be may look serene but the fishing is wild**

330 | **The unique landscape of Tsarabanjina**

329
Savagery beneath the surface
Nosy Be, Madagascar
November to May
Giant trevally

In the language of the Malagasy, Nosy Be means "big island" and visitors will find it just off the northwestern coast of Madagascar, toward the top. While it made its name for producing sugar and oils used in perfume, these days it's mainly a resort island and offers some fantastic giant trevally (GT) fishing. What often strikes anglers here is the contrast between the placid, calm blue surface of the sea, and the whiplash savagery of the GTs beneath it as they twist and turn, chasing baits fished on, or just under, the surface. Heart-pounding fights beneath beautiful skies await.

330
Desert island perfection
Tsarabanjina, Madagascar
April to July
Sailfish

So remote is Tsarabanjina, that it is not an island that anyone visits on their way to somewhere else. In the 1990s, it was used as the location for British TV program *Girl Friday*, in which the English actress (and national treasure) Joanna Lumley survived alone on the island for nine days. Part of the Mitsio archipelago, this is one of *the* destinations for diving and snorkeling in the region, and this fabulous visibility also makes the area great for catching sailfish. Experienced charter skippers can help novices spot, and then catch, the fish of a lifetime.

331 | **The calm waters of the Morne Peninsula**

332 | **A Saint Brandon's bonefish**

331
Record-breaking billfish
Morne Peninsula, Mauritius
October to April
Billfish

This tiny volcanic island has a paradise-on-earth reputation thanks to its white sands, cerulean waters, and an extraordinary mix of waterfalls, rain forest, coral beaches, luxury resorts, and the Sir Seewoosagur Ramgoolam Botanical Gardens. The ocean floor drops off to 3,000 ft (914 m) within a mile (1.6 km) of shore and although there is plenty of food for hungry billfish, they will still be enticed by a nice dead skipjack bounced behind a boat. After that, boat and angler must work in harmony to get one to the side and released. The island record currently stands at 1,355 lbs (615 kg). You have been warned.

332
You'll believe a fish can fly
Saint Brandon's Atoll, Mauritius
**September to December and
April to June**
Bonefish, permit, giant trevally

This tiny group of fifty islands, 300 mi (483 km) north of Mauritius, has over 100 sq mi (259 sq km) of coral reef and has remained virtually untouched by "civilization." The only way in is by charter—about 36 hours of sailing and on the expensive side—but on arrival, you will quickly see what all the fuss is about. Incredible, clear saltwater flats full of permit, giant trevally, and bonefish; the last is one of the finest sportfish species in the world, noted for its extraordinary turn of speed, and the ultimate challenge for the fly-angler.

333
The scrappiest fish in the sea
Alphonse Atolls, Seychelles
October to December and February to May
Milkfish

Alphonse is one of three closely grouped islands that form this fisher's paradise. They share 15 sq mi (39 sq km) of white sand-flats and lagoons which mean that angling pressure is minimal. All the species are abundant but a specialty is the turbo-powered milkfish, one of the very top targets for the fly angler. These fish reach 40 lb (18 kg) and their shape, their forked tail, and their lack of lactic acid combine to make them the ultimate fighting machine. The Seychelles also offer staggering natural beauty and are the home of the giant Aldabra tortoises.

334
GT capital of the world
Cosmoledo Atoll, Seychelles
Late October to mid December, late February to late April
Giant trevally

"Cosmo" as it is called in the giant trevally (GT) world, really is the epicenter. Everything here is set up for the perfect GT experience with guiding staff beyond compare. You are fishing a huge white-sand lagoon surrounded by seven islands in a pristine wilderness. There is a vast amount of wading available, and the lagoon edges and channels offer sanctuary to the ferocious GT that simply hammer those flies. Looking for top-end GT-fishing? Cosmo is the place.

333 | **Alphonse is celebrated for its milkfish**

334 | **Catch GTs at the perfect lagoons at Cosmoledo**

335
Super grand slam Mecca

Denis Island, Seychelles
All year, but end of May to end of September
can see choppy water
Super grand slam

If there is one place on earth where the grand slam of
billfish, yellowfin tuna, dorado, and wahoo is eminently
possible in a single day, then it is here on the exclusive
waters that surround Denis Island. Trolling is a prime
method here but fly-fishing is always possible in the
clear waters. The fishing grounds are uniquely richly
structured offering a wealth of submarine habitats. It is
this fact that attracts such a vast variety of fish species and
makes Denis one of the world's great fishing locations.

335 | Fishing the flats is a
wondrous experience

336
Fabulous flats sport

Desroches Island, Seychelles
November to May
Bonefish

Stay at Desroches and you have access to the legendary flats at both St. Joseph's Atoll and those on Poivre and the neighboring South Island. This availability gives huge variety and while traveling times can be over forty minutes, the sheer amount of bonefish make every second worthwhile. Twenty-fish days are common and the average size is high too, around 4 lb (1.8 kg) with plenty double that. Desroches offers endless activities making this a great location for the angling family.

337 | **And away! This is the essence of permit sport**

337
Fly-fish for the elusive "fish of a thousand casts"

Poivre Atoll, Seychelles
All year
Indo-Pacific permit

Indo-Pacific permit are plentiful but wary, so they don't have the nickname of "fish of a thousand casts" for nothing. But land your fly in the right spot and you'll land plenty of these silver-sided beauties. The Seychelles caters to sportfishing, and you can find bait shops and plenty of lures, flies, rods, and line should you need to. Permit here can be caught in just a few feet of water, meaning much of the fishing can be done in waders or from shore.

338
Trout from the mountain kingdom

Rivers of the Mountain Kingdom, Lesotho

September to May

Brown trout, rainbow trout

The rivers that run from the Mountain Kingdom (which include the Makhaleng, the Khubelu, and the mighty Orange River) provide plenty of accessible fishing for anglers in search of big brown and rainbow trout. However, if you're prepared to do a bit of guided hiking then you can have sections of these pristine waters to yourself; and this lack of pressure from other anglers means the fishing is fabulous. The scenery here is as varied as it is extraordinary, and the angler who can tear themselves away from the river will see snow-tipped mountains, lush green valleys, and rocky, mountainous terrain.

338 | **Fabulous trout swim in the desolate and demanding rivers of the Mountain Kingdom**

339
Big coppers off the Cape
Cape Vidal, South Africa
December to September
Red steenbras

When young, the red steenbras lives up to its name and presents with a beautiful deep-red livery, which turns to a lovely shade of copper as the fish matures. It's the largest of the sea bream family, can live for around fifty years, and grows up to 154 lb (70 kg) by feeding on squid, crustaceans, reef fish, and smaller sea bream. It's also endemic to the seas between Cape Point and Sodwana Bay. One of the best ways to catch these big-mouthed apex predators is by using a nice piece of fresh squid. They can be caught from charter boats or straight off the beach.

340
Fishing for bars of gold
Orange River, South Africa
May to September
Largemouth yellowfish, smallmouth yellowfish

For a river surrounded by such spectacular scenery, fly-fishing on the Orange River—especially for yellowfish—is pleasantly sedate. Weighted flies cast into water where the bottom drops off work well, as do streamers—larger flies that are actively retrieved to mimic crayfish, leeches, and so on. The yellowfish itself looks rather like a tigerfish with all its teeth removed, and is liveried in an iridescent yellow-gold. It's also adept at using the current to its advantage when hooked, and even an average fish — between 5 and 8 lb (2.3 and 3.6 kg)—will fight hard for its size.

339 | The ultimate adrenaline rush

340 | The Orange River is set in glorious countryside

341
Up for an African challenge?
Spekboom River, Drakensberg Mountains,
South Africa
Spring and fall
Brown trout, rainbow trout

The Spekboom is one of the few streams in
South Africa where trout breed naturally
and freely. This challenging river runs fast
and hard in summer, then slow and steady
once the rains have passed; in either state,
the water has a rare clarity that makes
stalking a big brown or rainbow trout a
challenge for even the most experienced
fly-angler. Add high grass banks and trees
dipping their heads into the water, and fish
winkled out of the Spekboom are always
well-deserved.

342
An angler's retreat
Vaal River Lodge, near Potchefstroom,
South Africa
September to May
Carp

The perfect retreat for any angler who likes to
balance hard hours on the river bank with an
equal number of jacuzzis, spa treatments,
massages, and visits to the steam room, the
Vaal River Lodge sits on the banks of one of
the region's best carp rivers. The fish here are
beautifully-scaled, muscular, and full of fight,
and although the Vaal's no secret, the visiting
angler will usually be able to find a quiet
spot to themselves. Be sure to fish into the
evening—not only is this a great time to
catch carp, but the sunsets are gorgeous too.

342 | **The dramatic Vaal Dam is perhaps South Africa's most dynamic carp fishery**

343

A beach vacation with added shark

Skeleton Coast, Namibia
September to April
Bronze whaler sharks

Shark-fishing from a boat is something, shark-fishing from the beach is something else. Although there are a number of different species found along the Skeleton Coast, the ultimate aim is the bronze whaler, one of the hardest-fighting and easily capable of stripping 400 yd (366 m) of line from a reel. To catch one you'll need patience, stamina, a rod like a telegraph pole, and a groin of steel (a fighting belt with a cushioned cup helps, but nevertheless . . .) and with luck one of these 100 lb (45 kg) plus beauties will oblige.

344

Where the river meets the sea

Kunene River mouth, Angola/Namibia
July to August
Kob, giant threadfin

In an area renowned for big tarpon, it's easy to forget that during July and August, when the tarpon are scarce, it's possible to catch one of Africa's more unusual fish—the giant threadfin. So-called because of sensitive, catfish-like whiskers that protrude from the pectoral area and help the fish locate food in muddy water. Threadfish can grow to 60 lb (27 kg) and give a terrific fight. The river mouth here is also home to a healthy population of kob, which grow to over 100 lb (45 kg) and look rather like oversized cod. Either species offer tremendous sport and are excellent table fish.

345

A magnet for Atlantic sailfish

Luanda, Angola
October to November
Atlantic sailfish

The capital city of Angola boasts a large
natural bay from which charters set sail in
search of Atlantic sailfish. Even as far back as
the 1970s, when the country was being torn
apart by the war of independence and the
civil war that followed, this was still a magnet
for anglers looking to challenge themselves
by catching one of the huge sailfish that
swim in these seas. Said to fight much harder
than their Pacific cousins, the Atlantic
sailfish here average around 70 lb (32 kg),
but fish above 100 lb (45 kg) are not
uncommon. Heavy line and a spinner is the
conservative tactic, but daredevils may also
wish to try their hand with fly-fishing tackle.

346

Big "jacks" right off the beach

Mussulo Beach, Luanda, Angola
November to March
Jack crevalle

It's a typical shoreline scene in west Africa—a
beautiful sandy beach stretching off into the
distance, crabs scuttling around everywhere,
local fishing-boats pulled up onto the beach,
and plenty of fish in the sea. No need for
subtlety here—a strong beach casting rod,
and a big spinner hurled out as far as
possible, and then cranked back in at speed
will often account for a big jack. They school
offshore, chasing small tuna for food, and
once one has been caught, more usually
follow. Expect a tough fight as even average
fish can weigh around 15 lb (6.8 kg).

343 | **The Skeleton Coast is as stark as its name implies but the fishing bursts with life**

Tigerfish at sunset

A tiger angler at work in the Okavango

Lure fishing is a favorite tiger approach, especially at low light

347

A mouth full of razors

Nxamaseri Island Lodge, Okavango
Delta, Botswana

Early September to mid-November

Tigerfish

It was once said of the tigerfish, "The tigerfish of Africa is the fiercest fish that swims. Let others hold forth as advocates for the mako shark, the barracudas, the piranha of the Amazon, or the blue fish of the Atlantic. To them, I say 'pish and tush.'" One glance at that mouthful of razor-sharp teeth—even on a small one—and the angler visiting this remote, exclusive lodge on the Okavango Delta, will be inclined to agree. The most exciting way to catch a tiger is on the fly, though spinners and lures work when the water is more colored.

348

BUCKET LIST FISH: Tigerfish and goliath tigerfish

CONGO RIVER, DEMOCRATIC REPUBLIC OF CONGO

Tigerfish is widely spread throughout Africa, but the aptly named, huge goliath is more restricted and the Congo River is one of its strongholds. A double-figure "tiger" (over 10 lb; 4.5 kg) is a good fish indeed, while the goliath strain can run to three figures (100 lb; 45 kg) of terrifying muscle . . . and teeth. Whatever the size, tigerfish of all weights are formidable adversaries. They fight desperately hard and their fangs can demolish the toughest of lures. Along with South American arapaima and Mongolian taimen, the goliath tigerfish is one of the three major trophies in world-fishing today.

The tigerfish is as fearsome as its name suggests—and more so in the case of the aptly named goliath

349 | The Congo River, seen here in all its fury, is one of the last homes of the goliath tigerfish

349
The real river monster
Congo River, Kinshasa, Democratic Republic of the Congo
June to October
Goliath tigerfish

Even for anglers who are familiar with the episode of the TV show *River Monsters*, when the presenter, Jeremy Wade, talks about the teeth of the goliath tigerfish and how they can take lumps out of other fish, out of crocodiles, and even out of people, it will still be a shock to see the real thing. The mouth of this fish is a horror-show of gruesome fangs, capable of taking lumps out of . . . well, you get the idea. Use brightly colored lures and spoons, live or cut baits—and definitely don't forget the wire leader.

350
Catch tarpon in a wildlife paradise
Setté Cama, Gabon
September to April
Tarpon

This village sits between the Atlantic ocean and the extraordinary Ndogo Lagoon, home to around 350 islands and crammed full of jack crevalle, snapper, threadfin, barracuda, and tarpon. It also marks the southern boundary of the Loango National Park, home to an amazing array of wildlife; there's an online video of a great tusker elephant walking and swimming across the lagoon that has been viewed nearly 4.5 million times. There are many different ways to fish for tarpon—the so-called "silver kings"—but the most thrilling is to sight-fish using a fly; it can be hard work, but incredibly rewarding.

AFRICA AND THE MIDDLE EAST

352 | **The giant grouper is an awesome challenge, a creature from the prehistoric age**

351
Captainfish
Faro River, Garoua, Cameroon
January to mid-March
Nile perch

Known by the locals as The Captain, Faro River has Nile perch that seem to come from a different angling planet. This is a raw experience, where lions call, where you wade croc-infested waters, and where elephants can force you off your beat. The fishing too is brutal. Almost exclusively fly-fishing, generally done at night when the big fish feed. But if you are up for it, this is a challenge beyond compare. It also represents an example of how sportfishing can bring tourist money to an area and persuade poachers that guiding is a better long-term lifestyle choice than illegally killing fish for market.

352
The bounty and beauty of Banana Island
Banana Island, Sierra Leone
November to May
Dorado, grouper, black marlin

The number of wrecked ships off the coast of Banana Island is testimony to the hazardous waters in Yawri Bay. Fortunately for anglers, they also provide a refuge—and fertile hunting ground—for a wide range of sportfish. The rocky bottom here, closer to shore, is ideal for grouper, while farther out you're likely to find dorado and black marlin. Trolling is still the most popular method, but increasing numbers of fly fishers are also discovering the aquatic bounty and beauty of Banana Island.

353
Tales from Tarpon Island
Sulima to Sherbro Island, Sierra Leone
January to May
Tarpon, snapper, leerfish

This section of the Sierra Leone coast—and specifically Sherbro Island—has earned its reputation as one of the world's premier tarpon fisheries, including at one time, nine world records. Growing to nearly 300 lb (136 kg) and looking like a herring that's been giant-sized by a mad scientist, these tough-fighting fish have all the tricks in their repertoire. Experienced tarpon anglers always prefer to hook a "jumper" rather than one that holds deep and uses the tide and current to its advantage—jumpers tire more quickly. And if the tarpon aren't showing, expect plenty of action from snappers and leerfish—the latter an underrated scrapper that's quick and has loads of stamina.

354
Playing a guitarfish
Acunda Island, Bijagos archipelago, Guinea-Bissau
December to January
Guitarfish, rays

Guitarfish, so-called because their bodies are shaped like a guitar— probably a Gibson SG rather than a Fender Strat—love sandy bottoms in temperate coastal waters, so Acunda Island is an almost perfect environment for them and other members of the ray family. When they're not cruising for food, they lie buried in the sand up to their eyes. Watching one stir into action from this seemingly torpid state, shrugging off the accumulated sand as it rises to a bait, is a wonderful sight.

354 | A hooked guitarfish pulls an angler's string harder than you'd ever believe possible

355 | Sailfish are acrobats in the air when hooked but breathtakingly balletic underwater

355
Majestic fishing on a "hidden" African archipelago
Bijagos Islands, Guinea-Bissau
October to May
Atlantic sailfish

This little-known coastal archipelago sits about 30 mi (48 km) off the mainland of Guinea-Bissau and is made up of eighty-eight islands, only 25 percent of which are inhabited all year. Having resisted the Portuguese colonizers for far longer than the mainland, these islands have retained many of their cultural traditions and animistic faiths. A UNESCO Biosphere Reserve since 1996, the archipelago nevertheless supports a thriving sportfishing industry with the mighty Atlantic sailfish—average length 7.5 ft (2.3 m) and weighing around 50 lb (22.5 kg)—at its heart.

356
Cassava and captainfish
Bakau Coast, Gambia
August to January
Cassava croaker, giant African threadfin

The country of Gambia is spread around the exotic Gambia River; this system is known for its diverse ecosystem and abundant wildlife. Down the coast, south of the river estuary, you find Bakau, and not far off its beach there are some interesting reefs with many types of big and strong fish. The target fish here are usually cassava, threadfin (captainfish), and sometimes African red snapper. It is easy to anchor up on the reef, and bottom-fish for these fighting beasts. The most effective bait is a live sardine on a single hook.

357
Beach bonanza
Batukunku Beach, Gambia
September to April
Common guitarfish, stingrays, prickly puffer,
African red snapper, grunts, sea catfish

Barda Konku beach lies one hour's drive
from Bakau. It is secluded, far away from
bathing tourists, and it has a couple of
reefs stretching out from the beach.
The best time, by far, is to fish on an
incoming tide, when the bigger fish
come in and search for food. Beach
casting with sand-grip-sinkers is a very
effective way to get to the fish, placing
the rods in rod holders. Most fish love
shrimp, and it is no different here; string
three or four shrimp up the line and end
it with a piece of fish on the hook, and
get ready to be busy.

A hedgehog or a puffer fish from Batukunka Beach?

The vast array of species here makes for a real adventure

A fabulous guitarfish beached at last after a long battle

358

Vacation resort monsters

Gambia River mouth, Gambia

All year, but best October to May

Guitarfish, stingray, captainfish

The Gambia River mouth is a huge sheet of water
from where you can catch glimpses of Senegal in
the distance. On average it's 10 to 100 ft (3 to 30 m)
deep and has noticeable tidal influences. This is all
about beach-casting and getting fish-baits well out
into the channel. All three species grow massive here
and fight with submarine power—it is not unknown for
220 lb (100 kg) anglers to be pulled down the sand and
into the surf by unseen monsters. The adventure is part
of the fun. The weather is great, the sands are alluring,
and there are plenty of bars to buy a beer while you wait.

**358 | Locals and tourists fish cheek by jowl
on the sands of the Gambia River mouth**

359
African silver kings
Gambia River mouth, Gambia
October to May
Tarpon

Tarpon flock here in the winter, and there are huge gatherings of fish reaching 300 lb (136 kg) around the estuary. A good skipper is key. The best fishing is half an hour either side of high tide, when you'll see superb fish rolling, taking in air, and hunting prey. Pods are nomadic too—an amazing spot one day can be fishless the next. Between May and September smaller tarpon move in large schools close to the shore and fish up to 60 lb (27 kg) can be taken by fly.

360
Endless sport
Gambian inshore reefs, Gambia
All year
Barracuda, snapper, jacks, grouper

The inshore reefs, sandbars, and wrecks here offer entertaining sea-fishing. There are sixty, perhaps even seventy, species up for grabs and catching a dozen or more in a day is not uncommon. Fish fresh shrimp for bait and you won't have a clue what the next bite could bring. Go heavier and you're in with a chance of a captainfish, barracuda, or ray. A good crew will advise you on techniques to use as tidal flows and water colors dictate.

360 | **Barracuda on the prowl, eyeing up their prey**

361
Wahoo: from sea to table
Santo Antão island, Cape Verde
December to May
Wahoo

Off the rocky northeastern coast of Santo Antão, the most northerly of the Cape Verde islands, you'll find wahoo fishing that is the stuff of dreams. These streamlined slabs of muscle are fast-growing school fish and can reach 8 ft (2.4 m) in length and 140 lb (64 kg) plus in weight; they're good eating too, the meaty texture responds well to baking and broiling. For a special treat, try rolling wahoo steaks in sesame seeds and then frying them for about a minute on each side; don't overcook though, or they'll go dry.

362
Gateway to the Atlantic blue marlin
São Vicente and Santiago islands, Cape Verde
March to July
Atlantic blue marlin

The marlin-rich waters around the islands of São Vicente and Santiago draw anglers from all over the world to enjoy what many believe is the ultimate marlin experience. It was here, after all, that a behemoth of 1,093 lb (496 kg) was landed in 1998, and as the sportfishing industry has developed since then, you can expect to encounter fish between 200 and 350 lb (113 and 159 kg) with a chance of hooking into something nearly double that. This island-fishing is particularly novice-friendly and boats will provide both tackle and bait for anyone who doesn't fish regularly.

361 | **The sleek wahoo is all fin and muscle**

362–363 | **Welcome to Cape Verde**

363
We're going to need a bigger boat . . .
Cape Verde
March to July
Blue marlin

There's an English folk song called "The Bristol Slaver" that goes: "Off Cape Verde we lay at anchor/Crammed from stem to stern/ Soon we sail to Kingston/Torn away from Africa, never to return." Infamous for its part in shipping slaves from West Africa to work in plantations in the Caribbean, North America, and Brazil, and for its place as a hub for traded goods coming the other way, echoes of Cape Verde's brutal past are all around. Today these islands, strung 380 mi (612 km) off the Senegal coast, are a world-class destination for blue marlin and a premier destination for anglers in search of monsters.

364
The sea awash with yellowfin tuna
Cape Verde
July to November
Yellowfin tuna

Weighing up to 450 lb (204 kg)? Check. Body like a torpedo? Check. Dark blue backs to blend in with the sea, yellow sides, and silver underbelly? Check. Delicious to eat? Check. There are few better ways to spend a day than fishing for the plentiful yellowfins that inhabit the waters around Cape Verde. Once you hit a school, the sport is likely to be fast and furious and many an angler returns from a day's charter fishing wanting nothing more than a hot shower, a cold beer, and an early night.

364 | **A yellowfin tuna boat returns home**

ASIA

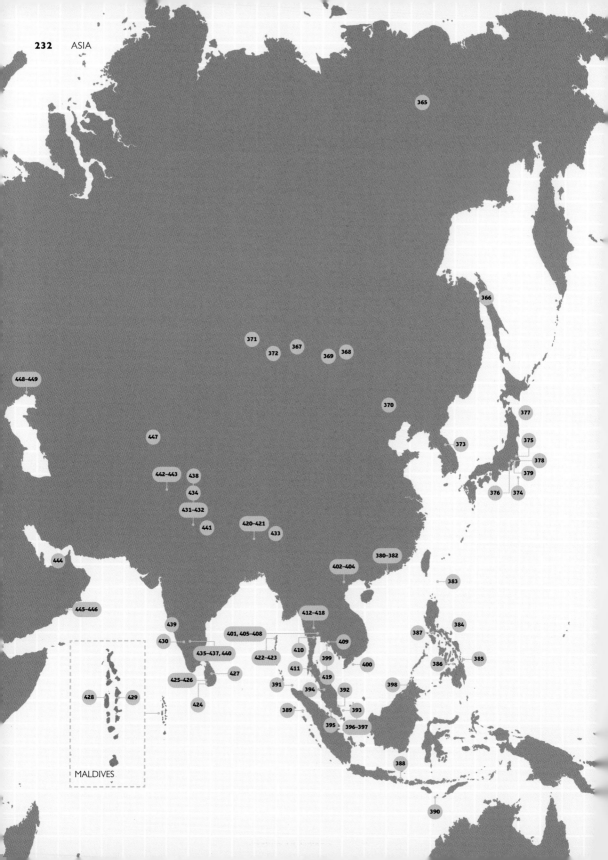

365

366

371
372   367
369 368

448–449

370

447   373
                                                         377
442–443 438   375
        434   378
431–432   379
        441   420–421   376 374
               433

444   380–382
                                          402–404
445–446   383

439   384
        412–418   387
430   401, 405–408   386   385
       435–437, 440   409
               410   398
       422–423   399
       411   400
425–426   419
427   392
391   394
428   429   389   393
        424   395 396–397
                           388

MALDIVES   390

ASIA: ENTRY LIST

365 Bolshoy Anwy River, Siberia, Russia
366 Sakhalin Island, Sea of Okhotsk, Russia
367 Borders of Mongolia and southeast Siberia
368 Onon River, Chinese border with Mongolia
369 Balj River, Khentii, Mongolia
370 Moron River, Mongolia
371 Shiskid River, Moron, Mongolia
372 Tengis River, a tributary of the Shiskid, Moron Province, Mongolia
373 Sancheoneo Ice Festival, Hwacheon, South Korea
374 Hachijō-jima, Tokyo, Japan
375 Kasumigaura and Shinotsu Lakes, Japan
376 Kawaguchiko Lake, Japan
377 Japan
378 Katsura and Sagami River, Fuji-Gozo region, Japan
379 Tokyo Bay, Japan
380 Aberdeen Harbour, Hong Kong, China
381 Happy Fish Farm, Tin Shui Wai, Hong Kong, China
382 Shek Pik Reservoir, Lantau Island, Hong Kong, China
383 Batan Island, Batanes, Philippines
384 Philippines
385 Siargao Island, Philippines
386 Camiguin Island, Philippines
387 Batangas, Philippines
388 Bali, Indonesia
389 Ujung Batu Island, Banyak Islands, Indonesia
390 Little Dana Island, Indonesia
391 Rondo and Wey Islands, Aceh Province, Sumatra, Indonesia
392 Kuala Rompin, Pahang State, Malaysia
393 Pulau Aur and Tioman Islands, Malaysia
394 Temenggor Lake, Perak State, Malaysia
395 Yellow Water Dam, National Botanical Park, Malaysia
396 Tioman deep reefs, Pahang, Malaysia
397 Tioman shallow reefs, Pahang, Malaysia
398 Tuaran River, Borneo, Malaysia

399 Koh Kut, Gulf of Thailand, also Tioman Island, Pahang, Malaysia
400 914 Pier, Con Dao Island, Ba Ria–Vung Tau, Vietnam
401 Boon Mar Ponds, Thailand
402 Bo Sang Fishing Park, Chiangmai Mai, Vietnam
403 Nui Coc Lake, Thái Nguyên, Vietnam
404 Thái Nguyên Lake, Vietnam
405 Ban Me Reservoir, Bang Pakong, Thailand
406 Bang Pakong River, Chachoengsao, Thailand
407 Bung Sam Lan Lake, Chachoengsao, Thailand
408 Kamphaeng Saen Lake, Kamphaeng Phet, Thailand
409 Khlong Yai Dam, Rayong, Thailand
410 Mae Klong River, Samut Songkhram, Thailand
411 Gilham's Fishing Resort, Thailand
412 Sri Nakarin Reservoir, Kanchanaburi, Thailand
413 Sri Nakarin Reservoir, Kanchanaburi, Thailand
414 Sri Nakarin Lake and rivers, Kanchanaburi, Thailand
415 Wai Ka Kaeng River, Sri Nakarin Reservoir, Kanchanaburi, Thailand
416 Sri Nakarin Dam, Kanchanaburi Province, Thailand
417 Sri Nakarin Dam, Kanchanaburi Province, Thailand
418 Khao Laem Reservoir, Kanchanaburi, Thailand
419 Ko Kut, Gulf of Thailand, Thailand
420 Bumthang River, Bumthang District, Bhutan
421 Sun Kosh River, Bhutan
422 Swaraj Island (previously Havelock Island), Andaman Islands, India
423 Havelock Island, Andaman Islands
424 Hikkaduwa, Southern Province, Sri Lanka
425 Lake Bolgoda, Colombo, Sri Lanka
426 Panadura Harbour, Colombo, Sri Lanka
427 Lake Polonnaruwa, North Central Province, Sri Lanka
428 Maamendhoo, Gaafu Alif Atoll, Maldives
429 Malé, Maldives

430 Kaveri River, Coorg, India
431 Western Ramganga River, Uttarakhand, India
432 Junction of the rivers Saryu and Kali, Pancheswar, India
433 Arunachal Pradesh, India
434 Ganges River, Byas Ghat, Haridwar, India
435 Galibore, Kaveri River, Karnataka, India
436 Galibore, Kaveri River, Karnataka, India
437 Cauvery River, India
438 Ramganga River, Jim Corbett National Park, India
439 West Coast, Goa, India
440 Kaveri River, Karnataka and Tamil Nadu, India
441 Karnali River, Nepal
442 Lidder River, Kashmir
443 Alpine lakes, Sonamarg, Kashmir
444 Persian Gulf, Dubai, UAE
445 Salalah, Dhofar, Oman
446 Shuwaymiyah, Oman
447 Mountain rivers of Kyrgyzstan
448 The Ural Delta, Gureyev, Kazakhstan
449 Ural River, Kazakhstan

365 | **Lenok trout fight hard, look spectacular, and often provide food out in the wilds of Central Asia**

365
Enjoy superlative fishing
Bolshoy Anwy River, Siberia, Russia
May to September
Lenok trout

Some anglers claim that trout fishing in eastern Siberia is the best in the world. Lenok trout are plentiful, and their appetite makes them a fun sportfish— cast pretty much anything at the right time and expect a hit. They're also a beautiful fish, a distant relative of the rainbow and just as pretty. Embracing the quiet solitude among the verdant spring greens and cotton clouds above is what fishing here in Siberia is all about.

366
The ultimate taimen adventure
Sakhalin Island, Sea of Okhotsk, Russia
Summer
Sea-run taimen

Even in the age of the internet, barely anything is known about the sea-run taimen in the far east of Siberia. While the species is on the IUCN Red List of Threatened Species, there are undoubtedly rod-caught specimens fished for annually and legally. Original reports were that the fish were, in the main, small. Recently, highly proficient anglers have landed gigantic trophies both in rivers like the Tym and in sea lagoons. Fish stocks must always come first and it's important to show 100 percent regard for conservation. However, if selective sportfishing can be done to help scientific research and local communities financially, then this is one of the ultimate adventures of the world today.

367
Mystery trout at the ends of the earth
Borders of Mongolia and southeast Siberia
July to September
Lenok trout, taimen

There is a vast region south of Lake Baykal which is rich in rivers but all but unexplored by sportfishers. The Ulan Moron River runs into the Selenga River, which crosses into Siberia, but because of the political situation it makes sense to keep your focus to the south, in Mongolia itself. Rumors abound of massive taimen and lenok trout way over 10 lb (4.5 kg) in weight. Lenok can be taken on a fly or lure and these rivers are prolific with fish averaging 5 lb (2.3 kg). It is a region of extraordinary wild beauty, still the haunt of bear, wolves, and nomadic hunters.

368
Fabled pike of the far east
Onon River, Chinese border with Mongolia
May to October
Amur pike

The river Onon empties into the vast Amur system that gives these rarest of pike their name. Very few western anglers have caught, or even seen more than a handful of photographs of, these pike that sport black-brown spots on a tawny background, making them look somewhat like leopards with fins. Fish for them with usual lure tactics in lagoons and backwaters off the main river, which is huge. This is wild terrain and wolf territory, a land where snow can fall in the summer. It's not a trip for the timid.

367 | The borders of Mongolia are wild, lonely, and untamed, the perfect location for a fishing adventure

369 | **The Balj National Park is crossed by rivers which hold extraordinary fish**

369
Amur treats
Balj River, Khentii, Mongolia
All year, but best August to October
Amur trout, black-spotted lenok

In the great Amur system, the rivers Onon and Balj meet in Genghis Khan's birthplace. These rivers hold, most famously, the fearsome taimen, but also a number of other species such as catfish, trout, redfin asp, and the magnificent Amur trout. This fish is closely related to the common lenok; they look similar except the Amur trout has clearly defined black spots all over its body. Both are plentiful in the Onon–Balj system. They are great sport fish, good fighters, and they happily take spinners as well as flies.

370
An overlooked wonder of a fish
Xar Moron River, Mongolia
July to late September
Lenok trout

While you can fish the Xar Moron River for lenok, in truth this species is found throughout Mongolia, Siberia, and even into Korea and China. This "trout of Asia" is so widespread it can be undervalued; but it is colorful, hard-fighting, and grows to close on 15 lb (6.8 kg). It is a hungry species and has to work hard for enough food to last it through the cripplingly cold winters. All flies work well including, perhaps especially, large lure patterns worked through deeper pools.

371

Salmonids in the heart of Asia
Shiskid River, Moron, Mongolia
July to late September
Taimen

This huge river joins the Yenisey basin and flows huge distances through Siberia to empty into the Kara Sea. The mighty, orange-tailed taimen that inhabit the system are equally large and dramatic. These land-locked salmonids are the top of the food chain and grow 4–5 ft (1.2–1.5 m) long. The main Shiskid is a surging torrent and the trick is to find the backwaters where you can fish by fly (9 or 10 wt recommended) or lure for these monsters. Keep mobile and travel through the boundless forests on foot or by horse to get the best out of a unique experience.

372

Grayling in coats of many colors
Tengis River, a tributary of the Shiskid, Moron Province, Mongolia
July to late September
Mongolian grayling

These rainbow-colored grayling are a unique subspecies and their beauty reflects the pristine river that is their home. Running through pine forests and snow-capped mountains, the Tengis flows as clear as any river on earth. Travel light and fish all the pools with a selection of brown and black nymphs, heavily leaded and tied to a tippet of 3-pound line. This is an empty landscape shared by wolves, bears, nomadic hunters, and, perhaps, the ghost of Ghengis Khan.

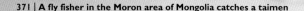

371 | **A fly fisher in the Moron area of Mongolia catches a taimen**

Whatever your age you must wrap up warm

Celebrate every catch

Getting ready to catch trout by hand—you've never tickled trout like this

373
Ice-fish among throngs of partying Koreans
Sancheoneo Ice Festival, Hwacheon, South Korea
January to February
Mountain trout

This mega-event in South Korea happens every winter, and is not your average fishing expedition. At the Sancheoneo festival, hundreds of people of all types and ages, from families with toddlers to grandparent couples to kids on a date, put on mittens and hats and try their hand at ice fishing once the river ice gets thick enough. There's even an arena where you can try catching trout by hand. Not exactly what most anglers dream of, but a one-of-a-kind fish festival nonetheless.

374

Catch yellowfin tuna in the sushi capital of the world

Hachijō-jima, Tokyo, Japan
September to November
Yellowfin tuna

The warm waters around this island off the coast of Tokyo are excellent sportfishing for a variety of fish, including yellowtail. These beauties come to feed on the variety of other smaller fish that come due to current upwellings near the island, meaning that you don't have to travel far to start casting your line. In the evenings, you can soak your cares away in the soothing warmth of one of the island's many thermal springs, or visit atmospheric temples and shrines.

375

Serious top water fun

Kasumigaura and Shinotsu Lakes, Japan
Winter for clear water and ice-fishing
Largemouth bass

Kasumigaura is the second biggest lake in Japan at 84 sq mi (220 sq km) and is famous for its traditional, huge-sailed trawlers called hobikisen. The lake is only an hour from Tokyo and there are plentiful boats to take you out, generally found along the western shore. Shinotsu Lake is equally accessible from Tokyo and is a favorite ice-fishing destination in the winter both for rainbow trout and for local fish.

376

A Mount Fuji experience

Kawaguchiko Lake, Japan
All year, best from July to October
Largemouth bass

There are five lakes in this region to the north of Mount Fuji, but Kawaguchiko is the largest, the most accessible, and the water that is most often fished. There is activity all year on the lake but summer is the best period for the bass and for a population of rainbow trout. On the north shore there are tackle shops and local guides, many of whom work out of Wilderness Lake Lodge where you will find guidance. Good fishing and wonderful Mount Fuji always in your sights.

375 | Fishing on Lake Shinotsu is an experience

377
BUCKET LIST FISH: Tuna
JAPAN

There are many members of the extended tuna family, such as the yellowfin, the albacore, and the skipjack, all of which offer superb fishing opportunities, but the bluefin is the prize of them all. The bluefin tuna has a vast range across the North Atlantic, the Pacific, and the Indian Oceans and can grow to a staggering 1,000 lb (454 kg) and more.

Smaller fish hunt and travel in large schools, but the monsters can be found in pods, typically chasing herring schools. When the seas explode with escaping prey fish, a trolled bait can be hammered and the fight of a lifetime could begin . . . these huge fish don't just have bulk, they can also swim at over 60 mph (100 km/h).

Fish from the tuna family have excited anglers for centuries; their size, beauty, and power never fail to thrill

379 | **As the sun sets over Tokyo Bay, the sea bass go on the rampage**

378

Perfection the Tenkara way

Katsura and Sagami rivers, Fuji-Gozo region, Japan
Summer and fall
Rainbow and yamame trout

These rivers are small, shallow, and crystal clear for the most part. They hold two kinds of trout and a char species and are very popular destinations. They are cradles of the Tenkara style of fly-fishing—a technique many have heard of but know little about. This is the place to learn; in Japan itself. A long rod, a long line, and no reel and the key is to place the fly on super-sensitive water with virtually no disturbance whatsoever.

380

Your sea adventure begins here

Aberdeen Harbour, Hong Kong, China
March or April to September or October depending on wind conditions
Tuna and wahoo

Aberdeen Harbour is an excellent base to find charter boats and knowledgeable skippers. Most fishing is done 20 to 40 nautical mi (37 to 74 km) offshore and trolling artificial lures is the most commonly used method. Six species of tuna are caught along with dorado, barracuda, amberjack, and even black and striped marlin.

379

City sport beyond compare

Tokyo Bay, Japan
October, late November
Japanese sea bass

Come fall, sea bass swarm into the shallow waters of Tokyo Bay in huge numbers. Action can be furious with fish averaging 2 to 6 lb (0.9 to 2.7 kg) with occasional monsters of 14 lb (6.4 kg) or more—all beautiful with a golden-bronze sheen. Virtually all lure types work, but keep changing until you find what works on the day. Fish around the docks with the Gate Bridge and the city skyline as a backdrop. One tip: going out at night can be dramatically successful.

381 | **Tilapia are bejeweled beauties**

382 | **The dramatic Shek Pik Reservoir**

381

Terriers of fish

Happy Fish Farm, Tin Shui Wai,
Hong Kong, China
All year
Carp, tilapia, pacu

This is the ultimate commercial water but
it is close to everything in Hong Kong and
offers escape and a fishing fix. You can even
hire gear there so it's perfect for a few hours
one evening. Tilapia are pretty much
guaranteed as are carp, probably commons
but with rumors of grass varieties, to perhaps
10 lb (4.5 kg). There are almost certainly
pacu in the water, which are sensational
fighters and worth the visit in themselves.
As for the rumored alligator gar? You'll have
to see for yourself!

382

Cracking carp close to civilization

Shek Pik Reservoir, Lantau Island,
Hong Kong, China
September to March
Carp, jewel fish

Shek Pik is one of seventeen large reservoirs
in Hong Kong and fishing is tightly
controlled but productive. The water is large
and deep, and it pays to watch for feeding or
rolling fish rather than fishing blind. Some
of the better areas are comparatively remote
and it is wise to fish light and keep on the
move until fish are sighted. The lake is
surrounded by hills and forest and the area
is nationally important for rock carvings over
3,000 years old.

383
Find dolphinfish off the rugged coast of Batan Island
Batan Island, Batanes, Philippines
April and May
Dolphinfish

The remotest province of the Philippines, the archipelagic province of Batanes, is home to rugged landscapes, with sheer cliffs plunging into deep-blue waters and prized dolphinfish, also known as dorado, or mahi-mahi in the Pacific. Troll surface baits or use artificial lures, such as squid or live bait. The local inhabitants of Batan Island, the Ivatan, make bait out of fresh shrimp, following ancient fishing traditions that have been handed down from generation to generation.

383 | **Dolphinfish are a stunning catch**

Blood pumping drama is what marlin fishing is all about

384
BUCKET LIST FISH: Black, blue, and striped marlin
PHILIPPINES

These members of the billfish family really are the big hitters of the high seas. Blues and blacks of 1,000 lb (454 kg) are the dream trophy, and striped aren't all that far behind in weight—and certainly not in fighting prowess. Blues can be found pretty much worldwide, while the blacks and striped are more confined to the Pacific and Indian Oceans. Wherever they are found, whether they are caught trolling, with bait or fly, these fish are the kings of the oceans and present one of angling's most exhilarating experiences. Strap yourself in and prepare for the battle of your life.

385
Surfing makes way for fishing
Siargao Island, Philippines
March to early May
Sailfish and marlin

Siargao Island is a sportfishing paradise for sailfish and marlin, especially in the spring, but it's a year-round venue for other species. It is one of around 7,000 islands that make up the country and was made famous by surfers pursuing the legendary Cloud 9 wave. However, from 2008, fishing was also promoted when the annual International Game Fishing Tournament was inaugurated. The port of General Luna is a center of operations and deep water can be found just 1 mi (1.6 km) out of the harbor.

385 | **A sailfish looks glorious in its fighting colors**

386
Spot fearsome barracudas in the shallows
Camiguin Island, Philippines
All year, but best December to August
Barracuda

Washed by strong currents, the small volcanic island of Camiguin is one of the country's best spots to fish for barracuda, wahoo, and giant trevally. Renowned for their aggressive behavior, barracudas are usually found in shallow waters— you can often spot them waiting in ambush or stalking small baitfish. Use light tackle spinning gear and artificial lures such as deceiver flies or poppers.

386 | **The waters around Camiguin Island**

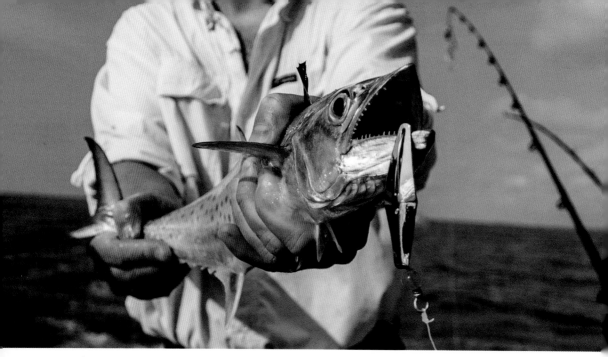

387 | **A large silver lure proved the downfall for this splendid Spanish mackerel**

387
Float live bait for ferocious predators
Batangas, Philippines
March and April
Spanish mackerel

The Spanish mackerel, known locally as tanigue, is the signature catch of Batangas. These predatory, finicky fish, with razor-sharp teeth, are particularly quick swimmers, making fast-moving lures the best choice—their teeth can slice through the line so make sure you use steel wire. They tend to feed on sardines, herring, and glass minnows—use plugs that mimic their prey, matching the color with the water color and forage. Be prepared for a vicious fight; they recklessly attack lures and flies. They're also particularly tasty, making for excellent table fare.

388
Catch monster-sized amberjack in Bali's gorgeous waters
Bali, Indonesia
October to May
Amberjack

Bali is a world-class tourist destination but it's got world-class sportfishing as well, and from October to May the seas are hopping with monster-sized amberjack, as well as many other prime sport fish. Nicknamed "sea donkeys" for their incredible strength, amberjack will give you pound-for-pound one of the best fights of any fish. Best of all, Bali is near shallow waters and shelves that drop thousands of feet, so great fishing isn't far away.

The reefs and sandbanks of Ujung Batu Island

A giant grouper can take a bait of massive size

Green turtles here benefit from protection initiatives

389

Experience pristine seas
Ujung Batu Island, Banyak Islands, Indonesia
January to July
Giant and humpback grouper

The giant groupers in these warm seas are prehistoric in their size and looks. They grow to colossal weights and live for fifty years, perhaps a lot more. Their eating qualities have led to huge exploitation and their numbers have decreased sharply in recent years. This is why it is such a privilege to fish for them in this vast nature park, an intensely protected area. Popping and jigging along the coral reefs is the method to lure these leviathans . . . watched by green and leatherback turtles as you do battle.

A fly-caught giant trevally is as exhilarating an adventure as angling can offer

390

BUCKET LIST FISH: Giant trevally

LITTLE DANA ISLAND, INDONESIA

The giant trevally—GT—really is the king of the reef system throughout both the Pacific and Indian oceans. It grows to 100 lb (45 kg) but specimens nowhere near that are still bruisers that make use of drop-offs, deep channels, and strong currents in battles that can give any angler a real beating. Their uniqueness lies in their ferocity, in the fact that they are so furious to feed that nothing, it seems, makes them afraid. They just have to attack any lure that comes into their field of vision, and as that will normally be a popper, that's where the fireworks begin. GT fishing in Indonesia is ever more popular.

391
A world GT hot spot
Rondo and Wey islands, Aceh
Province, Sumatra, Indonesia
April to November
Giant trevally

These superb islands are a
haven for giant trevally (GT)
but, in truth, the vast variety
of water types and the
remoteness of the islands
results in many species
making this their home.
Along with GT, trolling,
popping, and jigging will
attract sailfish, most tuna
varieties, marlin, snapper,
grouper, and amberjack—
among others. In fact, many
trophy hunters would rate
these islands in their top five
locations worldwide.

392
Sailfish in shallow waters
Kuala Rompin, Pahang State,
Malaysia
March to October
Sailfish

Sailfishing is so often an
all-day endeavor, with much
of it spent trucking to and
from the fishing ground.
Not so at Kuala Rompin, as
the island is smack in the
middle of prime sailfishing
territory. Mostly found in
shallow waters, the sailfish
can even be caught with
fly rods! But trolling or
jig-casting is common, too.
Regardless of the method
you use, you'll love the ease
and access to great fishing at
Kuala Rompin.

393
All blue sea species
Pulau Aur and Tioman islands,
Malaysia
**Mid-March to end
of October**
Black marlin, sailfish, wahoo,
cobia, grouper, Spanish
mackerel

There are many reasons the
fishing here is so sensational:
there is no commercial
fishing, the terrain is rocky
with islands dotted above
and below the waterline;
there are wrecks; and bait
fish like sardines proliferate.
There is an abundance of
black marlin, sailfish, wahoo,
cobia, grouper, Spanish
mackerel, and more.
Experienced skippers work
here. The preferred method
is to drift over structure,
jigging artificial baits.

393 | **The lack of commercial fishing at Pulau Aur makes for great sport**

A once-in-a-lifetime sighting of a Malaysian tiger

Pygmy elephants roam the thick jungle

Temenggor Lake holds stocks of giant snakehead

After a long fight, a snakehead hits the net

394

A lost paradise

Temenggor Lake, Perak State, Malaysia

December to March

Giant snakehead

This is a huge water covering 58 sq mi (150 sq km) and dotted with seventy islands. The best area is to the north in the protected Royal Belum zone. Here you will find serious and numerous giant snakehead, regularly reaching 40 lb (18 kg). Fish using all the usual methods close to snags and structures but also try frog imitations for snakeheads seen rising in open water. The lake is surrounded by ancient rain forest and there is always a chance of seeing elephant, Sumatran rhino, and even Malaysian tiger. Truly a lost paradise.

395
Park yourself here
Yellow Water Dam, National Botanical
Park, Malaysia
March to October
Pacu

The quarry here is the dramatic red-bellied
pacu, a native of South America but an
import that has settled well. Pacu are an
insanely hard-fighting fish and the preferred
method here is fly-fishing for maximum
excitement. Bait is allowed but only one rod
can be used and the fish reputedly run well
into double figures. This is a lovely place to
spend the day. There are several different
gardens in the park and the peace and
serenity around the dam are the perfect
antidote to the hustle and bustle of Kuala
Lumpur center just 20 mi (32 km) away.

396
Deepwater fighters
Tioman deep Reefs, Pahang, Malaysia
March to October
African pompano, trevally, snappers,
groupers, lizardfish

An hour's boat-ride east of Pulau Tioman
there is a huge reef with a mix of bottom-
dwellers, like groupers and snappers, and
fast-movers, like trevally and pompano. The
reef is 200 ft (61 m) deep, and the best way
to get to the fish is with a lead weight and a
live mackerel, or squid. There are some great
big groupers that can be very difficult to land
because they dive into cracks in the reef,
before you have a chance to fight them up.
Sometimes you know you have hooked
something completely different when the
fish is shooting off, away from the reef, and
that is the ultra-fast trevally.

395 | **Yellow Water Dam provides a serene escape from the frenzy of the city**

397 | **A needlefish skips over the calm waters of the Indian Ocean**

Surface fireworks

Tioman shallow reefs, Pahang, Malaysia
April to August
Common dolphinfish, queenfish, needlefish,
barracuda, skipjack tuna, Spanish mackerel,
black marlin

The island of Pulau Tioman, situated 31
miles (50 km) off the east coast of the
Malaysian mainland, is a true, exotic gem;
lovely nature, unspoiled by tourists, rich
coral reefs, and many of the most interesting,
tropical, surface-hunting fish only a short
boat-ride away. Artificial reefs have been
constructed to attract baitfish, and of course
this in turn attracts the hunters. Dolphinfish,
barracudas, queenfish, needlefish, even
marlin, attack surface lures, Rapalas, and
spoons; and many of these fish fight almost
as much in the air as in the water.

Sound conservation going on

Tuaran River, Borneo, Malaysia
**February to June and September
to October**
Borneo mahseer

These fish are close cousins of the Indian
mahseer, though not quite as large. They
might only top 30 lb (13 kg) or so, but
they fight with all the brutal power you
would expect. Medium-weight lure or
fly-gear is called for, but above all travel
light. The key is to cast a couple of times
and move on. Good boots are essential.
Mahseer here have suffered from the
logging industry and wholesale poaching.
The Tagal System, a community-based
conservation approach, encourages
sportfishing and the employment of
fishing guides. It's an excellent initiative
every angler should encourage.

399

Feisty pickhandle barracuda are plentiful in these waters

Koh Kut, Gulf of Thailand, also Tioman Island, Pahang, Malaysia

October to March

Pickhandle barracuda

These beautiful, fast fish are excellent fighters and catching one is a thrill of a lifetime, especially when you consider that you'll be fishing in one of the world's most beautiful landscapes. Talcum-powder-soft sand, towering coconut palms, verdant jungles, and azure flats all beckon the angler to enjoy some of fishing's finest. Look for the distinctive "pickhandle" marks on their sides to identify them.

400

Land impressive barracuda on an infamous prison island

914 Pier, Con Dao Island, Ba Ria–Vung Tau, Vietnam

May to October

Barracuda

Pier 914 is so named because of the 914 prisoners who were killed during the pier's construction. Today, this island is a tourist paradise, with great fishing for those who come to look for it. The island has inexpensive charters out to great reef fisheries, where barracuda are plentiful year-round, but choppy swell conditions make the summer months a better time to visit. Nighttime squid fishing off the pier is a popular pastime for tourists and locals as well.

This image of the battling barramundi explains its iconic status across half the world

401
BUCKET LIST FISH: Barramundi
BOON MAR PONDS, THAILAND

This exotic super-perch feeds in the coastal regions of Asia from the Persian Gulf to China and around the northern half of the Australian coast. You look for them in creeks, mangrove swamps, rivers and their estuaries where they feed on fish, crabs, and shrimp. These are buccaneering predators that just hammer into flies and lures alike and can grow to 100 lb (45 kg) or more of aggressive muscle that challenge angler's gear to the limits. Fish for them with stealth, maneuvring your boat close to structures, or small fish explosions on the surface, and then wait for the fireworks to begin.

402

The joy of park fishing

Bo Sang Fishing Park, Chiangmai Mai, Vietnam

All year, slower in winter

Mekong (striped) catfish

The concept of the Thai fishing parks began many years ago with the legendary Bung Sam Ran fishery. It was largely created because most Thai still waters had been pretty much fished out. Bo Sang is a great example of these venues with huge catfish available in comfortable and exotic surroundings. If it is large, dramatic, and hard fighting species that turn you on, then lakes like Bo Sang will give you immense pleasure.

403

Fish lurk in this popular lake

Nui Coc Lake, Thái Nguyên, Vietnam

March to September

Monster black carp

This picture-perfect lake offers tranquility and postcard vistas of Vietnam. It's popular for all sorts of reasons, but sportfishers should know that it holds a healthy population of the largest carp in the world. Monster black carp can reach sizes of 6 ft (1.8 m) here, and landing one is a feather in the cap of even the most experienced angler. Fishing tours run from several points, and casting from shore is possible.

404

The battling black carp of Asia

Thái Nguyên Lake, Vietnam

March to September

Black carp

This is a fantastic experience with fish of 60 lb (27 kg) plus that fight to within an inch of their lives. They are glorious to look at, and in the heat of summer, feeding activity is high. Spring is hot as well and schools gather in the shallows ready to spawn. Sight-fishing is popular and it pays to keep mobile. For bait use large (1 in; 22 mm) boilies or go local with live snails. It's often illegal to fish at night, so you can enjoy the nightlife, too.

405

Widespread popular sport fish

Ban Me Lake, Bang Pakong, Thailand

December to March

Barramundi

The barramundi is one of the best known sport fish, and one of the most targeted angling species. It is adaptable, thriving in freshwater, brackish water, and saltwater. In Thailand you can find it in some freshwater lakes, and one of them is Ban Me. They don't grow as big here as they do in saltwater, but there are still plenty over 20 lb (9 kg). The best bait here is whole saltwater fish, such as mackerels and scads.

407 | **Huge Siamese carp and catfish thrash the surface of Bung Sam Lan Lake**

406
Mammoth freshwater rays

Bang Pakong River, Chachoengsao, Thailand

January to June

Giant freshwater whipray, cowtail stingray, white-rimmed stingray

Marine rays grow big, but the freshwater versions are not small either. The Bang Pakong River holds some enormous freshwater species, of world record sizes—well over 1,100 lb (500 kg) and nearly 8 ft (2.5 m) in diameter. Nighttime boat-fishing is the best approach, but be prepared for heavy fights of up to eight hours. The best bait is live, giant prawn from the river itself.

407
Largest carp in the world

Bung Sam Lan Lake, Chachoengsao, Thailand

All year, except January

Giant barb (Siamese carp)

Bung Sam Lan is probably best known for its many big, native Mekong-catfish species and a number of South American giants like arapaima and redtail catfish. In essence, Bung Sam Lan is a glorified "Put and Take" lake, but it is a *must* to try when you are in Bangkok. Another native giant found here is the giant barb. It looks much like a weirdly colored, oversized common carp, but here the similarities end, because it grows to nearly 660 lb (300 kg). At Bung Sam Lan there are many big examples, and they can be caught all day, but definitely best at night, and best caught on bread with a bait sack.

408
Golden price
Kamphaeng Saen Lake, Kamphaeng Phet, Thailand
February to November
Isok barb (Jullien's golden carp)

The landscape here is jungle mixed with rice paddies, lakes, and small villages, and the people are always friendly. In these rural and wild regions, another of Thailand's enormous cyprinids can be found: the Isok barb. Big specimens are hard to find, but in Kamphaeng Saen Lake, there is a good number of fish of 20 lb (9 kg) or more; keeping in mind it can grow to 150 lb (68 kg). The seven-striped Isok barb is also immensely beautiful, with a golden base color, black stripes, and completely red eyes. It is best caught on a paste bait made of rice husk flour, called "*lam.*"

409
Fascinating fish in a lonesome lake
Khlong Yai Dam, Rayong, Thailand
July and August
Giant snakehead

This is a near 186 mi (300 km) trek from Bangkok but offers sensational sport with these voracious predators. A boat is necessary to reach the best locations, generally tucked away amid expanses of floating vegetation. Here the snakeheads lie in wait, preparing to ambush passing tilapia . . . or your lure. The action is sensational and the fish fight as they bid to regain the sanctuary of snags. Dawn, dusk, and cloudy days prove best.

409 | **Khlong Yai Dam is a must-fish venue for snakehead**

Seeing a monitor lizard is a privilege—but take care

A giant stingray ready to be released

The unreal beauty of Mae Klong River

410

Monster fish in a rugged setting

Mae Klong River, Samut Songkhram, Thailand
Dependent on tides and lunar periods
Giant freshwater stingray

This is serious. You are boat-fishing the great tidal reaches of the Mae Klong with 130 lb (59 kg) class gear and weights of 2 lb (0.9 kg) to keep the bait on the river bed. The giant rays can weigh 660 lb (300 kg) or more and can fight for hours in swift currents. While this is a grueling task, you are surrounded by the beauty of golden temples and sunsets with the ever-present chance of seeing dragon-like monitor lizards. A three-fish-a-day limit makes great conservation sense.

411

A laid-back monster experience

Gilham's Fishing Resort, Thailand

All year, best from May to mid-December

Mekong catfish

Now that these extraordinary catfish have become excruciatingly rare in the river that bears their name, Gilham's provides a viable, ecologically sustainable, alternative venue. Here, fish to 300 lb (136 kg) grow fast in the 12 acre (4.8 hectare) lake, along with other stars of the fish world such as arapaima to 500 lb (227 kg) and more, Siamese carp, and redtail catfish. In the neighboring small "beginners" lake there are also huge giant snakehead. Although not a wild adventure, this is an experience with some of the rarest fish on the planet.

412

Floating fun

Sri Nakarin Reservoir, Kanchanaburi, Thailand

December to March

Asian redtail catfish, striped wallago catfish

This huge reservoir is surrounded by dense jungle. It contains enormous amounts of fish and a variety of species, including a few of Thailand's largest freshwater fish, many of which reach weights of over 200 lb (90 kg). People live on the reservoir in floating communities and earn an income from fishing, foraging, and tourism. Fishing from the floating houses is fun and several species stay under them, such as striped wallago (helicopter) catfish and the otherwise elusive Asian redtail catfish, both of which grow to over 175 lb (79 kg). Most fish around the houses are caught with dead-fish baits.

412 | **The houseboats on the Sri Nakarin Reservoir attract fish and make for perfect fishing stations**

413 | A giant snakehead

414 | The peace at Sri Nakarin Lake belies the drama when a fish is hooked

413
Snakes and giant snakeheads
Sri Nakarin Reservoir, Kanchanaburi, Thailand
**July to September and December
to March**
Great snakehead, Indonesian snakehead

At Sri Nakarin it is not uncommon to come across a king cobra swimming on the surface, a scary encounter because it could jump into the boat and spoil your day. There are also other fierce snake-like creatures swimming around—the giant snakehead species. Two of these, the great snakehead and the Indonesian snakehead, are both capable of weighing over 45 lb (20 kg). They are extremely fierce hunters that defend their young aggresively. They are not afraid of anything, so the best baits are colorful and noisy surface-baits, highly visible Rapala lures, and flashy spinner-baits.

414
Unlikely giants
Sri Nakarin Reservoir and rivers,
Kanchanaburi, Thailand
December to March
Giant featherback, clown featherback

Sri Nakarin Reservoir and rivers are full of interesting fish, but one type is especially abundant, the weird and wonderful giant featherback. Featherbacks and other knifefish are often connected with the aquarium-fish trade. While they make super interesting aquarium fish, small and benign enough to keep, it is so wrong for the featherbacks. They are ferocious predators, which can grow to 60 in (152 cm), and well over 45 lb (20 kg). Featherbacks are opportunistic fish, taking live and dead prey, so they are actually not that hard to catch when you find them; but what a trophy when you do.

415

Elusive mahseer

Wai Ka Kaeng River, Sri Nakarin
Reservoir, Kanchanaburi, Thailand
December to March
Thai mahseer, greater brook carp

There are many small rivers running
in to Sri Nakarin Lake, and the Wai
Ka Kaeng is particularly beautiful.
More interestingly for the angler, it
has enough flow to attract one of
Thailand's most elusive and sought-
after fish, the Thai mahseer. Besides
its good looks, the mahseer is a highly
treasured sport fish because of their
fighting qualities. They hunt fish,
like true predators, so the best bait is
a live fish under a float, or free-lined
in the current.

416

Catch gargantuan giant featherbacks with an idyllic backdrop

Sri Nakarin Dam, Kanchanaburi, Thailand
All year
Giant featherback (knifefish)

As far as evolution goes, the giant featherback is
up there with the platypus as being one of those
creatures that seems made up of a bunch of other
animals' parts. The long anal fin, the odd hump-
shaped back, the tiny "feather" of a dorsal fin, they
all make for one strange-looking fish. The fact that
it can grow to 5 ft (1.5 m) long and weigh up to
50 lb (22.5 kg) makes it all the more worthy of
catching the next time you're in Thailand. The
surroundings are gorgeous, too: a series of
connected waterfalls, national parks, and the
dam itself make for a spectacular experience.

415 | Mahseer lie like battleships in the flow

416 | The beauty of Sri Nakarin Dam at sunrise

417
Land the curious-looking (and tasty) whisker sheatfish
Sri Nakarin Dam, Kanchanaburi, Thailand
All year
Whisker sheatfish

This beautiful dam, the lake behind it, the nearby national park, and the surrounding area hold a wealth of natural resource treasures, from stunning waterfalls to animals and plants you'll find nowhere else in the world. The waters though hold riches of another kind: plentiful whisker sheatfish, which grow to be some of the world's largest.

418
Thailand's "black bass"
Khao Laem Reservoir, Kanchanaburi, Thailand
September to March
Hampala barb

This huge reservoir near the border with Myanmar is situated in a national park, and contains an enormous amount of fish and fish species, besides the wild and exotic fauna and flora of Thai jungles. Khao Laem is best known for the giant snakehead species, including the hampala barb (also locally known as jungle perch). It is one of those fish species, like bass for example, which don't grow particularly big, but still captivate anglers for their fighting qualities, and in the case of the hampala barb, the aggressiveness with which it hunts and attacks artificial lures.

417 | **The azure waters of Sri Nakarin hold monster whisker sheatfish**

419

Squid boat adventures

Koh Kut, Gulf of Thailand, Thailand

All year

Sailfish, cobia, Spanish mackerel, whipray, parrotfish, grouper, snapper, sea bream

Koh Kut is a tropical Thai island some hours boat-ride from Trat Harbour. Koh Kut is best known for its tourism, just like Koh Chang, but the fishing here is another wonder of southeast Asia. Of all the ways to fish at Koh Kut, the ultimate experience is to stay on a squid-fishing boat for few days, and fish your heart out. Almost all fishing styles will work; bottom-fishing for cobia and whipray, surface-fishing for sailfish and queenfish, and light-tackle fishing for all sorts of groupers, snappers, sea bream, and batfish.

420

Fly-fish for brown trout in the shadow of the Himalayas

Bumthang River, Bumthang District, Bhutan

Mid-April to mid-May, October

Brown trout

Brown trout in Bumthang are a fisheries management success story, with decades-long stocking efforts resulting in a healthy brown trout population in many of Bhutan's streams and rivers. You can't beat the beauty of the Himalayas, which seem so close as to be crowding you, and in this remote, infrequently visited country you'll feel like you're the first person to visit there. Bring all the gear you'll need, as it's unlikely you'll find that odd thing you forgot in a local market.

419 | **The idyllic Koh Kut at sunset**

420 | **Trout fishing in Bhutan can be a spiritual event**

421

A mahseer Shangri-La
Sun Kosh River, Bhutan
Spring
Mahseer

Fishing in the magical kingdom of Bhutan is like stepping back in time. The Sun Kosh offers all-but-virgin fishing as it runs through primeval forest still roamed by elephant, tiger, and leopard. Trips into Bhutan are a rare privilege and the Sun Kosh is perhaps the best water in the world today for fly-fishing mahseer. Most of the fish are of the long, lean golden strain but there are rumors of the chocolate variety as well—a fish of almost unicorn rarity. This is a Shangri-La journey to a Buddhist stronghold that feeds the fisher's soul.

422

Troll or jig for giant barracuda in this far-off, idyllic isle
Swaraj Dweep (previously Havelock Island), Andaman Islands, India
October to May
Barracuda

The Andaman Islands offer some of the world's remotest sportfishing and thus, you're likely to catch huge fish. All the biggies are here: marlin, sailfish, tuna, amberjack, grouper. But barracuda fishing here is second to none, with massive fish that come to the large coral atolls that surround the island. No surprise, there is excellent swimming, snorkeling, and diving here too, making it a great fishing choice for the whole family, as there's plenty of alternate activities to do and sights to see.

421 | A fly-caught mahseer from the Sun Kosh river

423
Surface thrashing mayhem
Swaraj Dweep (previously Havelock Island),
Andaman Islands
October to May
Giant trevally

The seas around the Andamans are fertile
beyond belief and bristling with all the
sought-after marine species but it is perhaps
for giant trevally that they are legendary.
Swaraj Dweep is a perfect base and
connoisseurs have recently discovered the
unspoiled waters and huge numbers of these
fighting fish. The purist method is to fish
surface poppers once a school of scattering
prey fish has been spotted and takes are
volcanic. Watch white-bellied sea eagles fish
around you, as your boat explores the
Andaman reefs for action.

424
Choose your own adventure
Hikkaduwa, Southern Province, Sri Lanka
July to August, December to February
Barracuda, giant trevally

You don't need to motor for hours to
reach the fishery here in Hikkaduwa, since
the island is already in the midst of it all.
Find giant trevally and huge barracuda
lurking almost anywhere above the reef
or in the network of channels and flats
surrounding the coastline, and the outflow
from Hikkaduwa Lake, inland, means
big fish come in close to feed off the smaller
fish the nutrient-rich currents attract.

425

Golden fish from an island pearl

Lake Bolgoda, Colombo, Sri Lanka
All year
Barramundi

Bolgoda consists of two major water bodies covering an immense 144 sq mi (374 sq km). The water is fresh but with a slightly brackish content that attracts and nourishes forty fish species. Barramundi up to 3 ft (1 m) in length are the star attraction, especially as the location is only 10 mi (16 km) from the nation's capital out on the Galle road. Lure fishing is favored though big flies are successful when used. This beautiful fishing venue offers a truly convenient escape from city life.

426

Top city venue

Panadura Harbour, Colombo, Sri Lanka
November to April
Giant trevally

Little by little, the deeper-sea fishing around this jewel of an island is being recognized. Panadura is a well-known attraction and it is possible to get top-rate charters here. The giant trevally fishing is truly world class as it has been little exploited and surface popper work, the cream of the sport, can be electric. It does get hot and in the glaring sunlight around midday you can try jigging for plentiful alternative species such as dogtooth tuna and amberjack.

427
Hook some of the world's largest tilapia
Lake Polonnaruwa, North Central Province, Sri Lanka
All year
Tilapia

Tilapia is a fun fish to catch and puts on a good show for their size. If you fancy the beautiful shores of a destination that's well off many anglers' maps, consider booking your next trip out to Sri Lanka. Lake Polonnaruwa has several stunning resort locations, beautiful jungles, and tilapia that will put most other spots to shame. The ancient city of Polonnaruwa is a fascinating glimpse into the past if you need a break from fishing or there are some bad weather days.

427 | **The exquisite beauty of Lake Polonnaruwa is best appreciated early and late, when the fishing is best too**

428 | Hire a boat and get close to the biggest GTs

429 | Shark cruise the waters off Malé

428

Fly-fish in a remote island paradise

Maamendhoo, Gaafu Alif Atoll, Maldives

All year

Giant trevally

Land 40 to 80 lb (18 to 36 kg) GTs while slowly cruising the Maldives' vast network of channels, flats, and open water. If fly-fishing for these beauties is your thing, you'll be in seventh heaven, as it's easy to bring these "big game" fish to the surface. The fishing on the flats is generally smaller, but can be just as rewarding as pursuing larger catch farther away from shore.

429

You don't have to go far to find great grouper in Malé

Malé, Maldives

All year

Reef shark, grouper

Smack dab in the middle of the vast Indian Ocean, the Maldives have incredible sportfishing because they're right where the fish are. You won't be disappointed setting off from Malé's port and getting to great fishing before you've even lost sight of the land. This spectacular archipelago has flats, deep water, and everything in between, meaning your chances are great for catching whatever fish you're after. Grouper and reef shark are popular sportfishing choices here. It goes without saying the snorkeling here is also second to none.

431 | **Anglers cross the Ramganga River**

430

Last domain of the mighty golds

Kaveri River, Coorg, India
November to late March
Golden mahseer

The golden mahseer, the great half-carp, half-barbel of the subcontinent, is one of the legends of the angling world—a prize-fighter that lives on in a river that boils like a cauldron. Mahseer fishing with bait and lure is an addiction and while access to much of the Kaveri is disputed, evidence suggests there are monsters in excess of 100 lb (45 kg) to be caught around Coorg. Elephants, leopards, and crocodiles add to the adventure.

431

Primeval fish from a heavenly river

Western Ramganga River, Uttarakhand, India
May and June
Goonch catfish

The goonch is unique among the catfish family; its size is colossal, into the hundreds of pounds (over 50 kg) and its looks make a *Dr. Who* monster look commonplace. Fish with lures of deadbaits in the dark, mysterious pools and prepare for a hook-up with the bowels of the earth. You are in an area inhabited by tigers which gives the experience a sense of fantasy.

432

In the footsteps of the raj

Junction of the rivers Saryu and Kali, Pancheswar, India
April to June, September and October
Northern mahseer

This place is sacred to mahseer anglers. The method is once again lure fishing, often with big spoons and plugs; fishing down and across like you would do for salmon. Northern mahseer are sleeker than their southern, golden cousins and their speed in these mountainous streams is beyond belief. The best anglers in the world are drawn to this remote location by 60 lb (27 kg) of pure, sleek muscle in fish form. One of angling's ultimate challenges.

433

Legendary fish in the land of the gods
Arunachal Pradesh, India
After the monsoon
Chocolate mahseer

Could this be the most demanding trip in this book? This area is exceedingly remote and little is known about its rivers which feed into the Brahmaputra River. Expeditions have found extraordinary wildlife, but fish have been harder to locate. Mahseer, chocolate or golden, leave the river during the monsoon to spawn in the tributaries. You must intercept them as the rains cease and rivers fall. Get it wrong, and they are back in the vast Brahmaputra, impossible to locate.

434

Jewels of the Holy River
Ganges River, Byas Ghat, Haridwar, India
September to October
Northern mahseer

The river Nayar joins the Ganges at the village of Byas Ghat, right by the historic landmark of The Black Rock. This vast boulder sits in the parent river beneath the junction and has seen hundreds of mighty fish landed in its shadow over the last century. Lure fishing on this huge, holy river in the aftermath of the monsoon can be electrifying as the river drops and the fish reassemble after spawning. Logistics are not easy and the journey is long but feel the rush of that first 100 yd (91.4 m) run and know every moment has been worthwhile.

435

Indian predators
Galibore, Kaveri River, Karnataka, India
All year, but best November to April
Great snakehead, cobra snakehead, Pangas catfish, wallago catfish

This river is a classic thanks to the mahseer, but there are other hard-fighting fish here and serious predators. The cobra snakehead takes colorful and noisy surface baits while the wallago and Pangas catfish take just about anything. Restrictions are in place so check before going to this aquatic paradise.

436

Big jungle cyprinids
Galibore, Kaveri River, Karnataka, India
December to April
Korhi barb, pigmouth carp, labeo

The Korhi barb reaches well over 22 lb (10 kg). It often takes the same ragi-paste bait we use for mahseer, and it fights surprisingly hard even on mahseer tackle and gear. But it is, of course, even more fun catching these cyprinids on lighter tackle, and they happily take small ragi balls, worms, and pieces of fish.

A conservation team catch and release a golden mahseer

437
BUCKET LIST FISH: Mahseer
KAVERI RIVER, INDIA

There are many members of the mahseer family but the angler is most interested in the giant humpback mahseer of southern India and the more streamlined golden mahseer of the Himalayan regions and Myanmar. To an angler's eye, mahseer look half-carp and half-barbel and whether caught by fly, bait, or lure they rank in the top five world-trophy list. And when it comes to freshwater fighters, they are top of the list. The dream is a fish of 100 lb (45 kg) plus but their range has been affected by modern development and mahseer conservation has become a big issue this century.

438
Catch a tiger by the tail
Ramganga River, Jim Corbett National Park, India
**October to November and February
to May**
Mahseer

Hook a Ramganga mahseer and it can feel
like all the tigers in the world are on your
line, such is the ferocity of the fight. And of
course, if there is one expedition where a
face-to-face hook-up with a wild tiger is
possible, this is it. Jim Corbett National Park
and the area around it is a magical mix of
forest, mountains, and isolated villages. In
the clear waters of the river, the fishing is
electrifyingly thrilling, whether on lure or fly,
and the trekking is out of this world too—it
makes for a never-to-be-forgotten adventure.

439
Electric sport in gentle Goa
West Coast, Goa, India
October to December
Snappers, groupers, jacks, threadfin
salmon, barramundi

This truly is an Indian paradise for the
adventurous sea-angler. About 25 mi (40 km)
offshore, you'll find 160 ft (40 m) depths
where trolling both artificial and natural
baits produces kingfish, wahoo, cobia,
sailfish, dorado, jacks, tuna, and barracuda.
Inshore fishing around countless bays,
schools, and reefs is equally abundant and
here you'll catch snappers, groupers, jacks,
threadfin salmon, and even cracking
barramundi. The heat can be a problem and
inshore fishing is more productive early and
late in the day, especially after darkness falls.

439 | **Whether you catch a fish or not, the beach at
Goa is a wonderful place to be at sunset**

440

Go after the voracious "freshwater shark"

Kaveri River, Karnataka and Tamil Nadu, India
All year
Wallago (catfish), Pangas catfish

An apex predator of India's rivers, the wallago is one strange-looking fish. Its tentacles stick out like a lobster's, it has so many razor-sharp teeth its mouth looks like it's coated in fur, and it's so ferocious that it's called the "freshwater shark" by locals. Landing one is a challenge, but those who persevere will be rewarded with a great fight and the pride that comes from adding one of the world's prize fish to the bucket list.

441

Find the fabled golden mahseer

Karnali River, Nepal
February to April, October to November
Golden mahseer

The Karnali River, Nepal's largest and longest, is also its best for fishing. It's a paradisical spot, replete with freshwater dolphins surfacing nearby, crocodiles sunning themselves on warm mudbanks, and in the murky water, the golden mahseer waits for you to cast. These fish are fighters, prized for their cunning and ability to last until the end. Some grow around 6 ft (1.8 m) long. They're a great show fish, too, with gorgeous golden-red sides that look fantastic in photos.

440 | Indian rivers teem with catfish species

441 | The vast Karnali river is home to mahseer

443 | Catching trout in alpine lakes at 10,000 feet (3,000 metres) is a memorable experience

442

High altitude fly-fishing perfection

Lidder River, Kashmir
April to September
Trout

Brown trout were stocked into this serene valley over a century ago and now the river is cared for by guides and river guards to maintain the fish's presence. Outside monsoon time the river flows a glacial green in a series of volcanic rapids and deep, alluring pools. Above the waterline everything is forest and mountain. Camping allows you the flexibility to explore. The trout take most nymph patterns and occasionally come to the surface, though this is icy water at real altitude. One of the great fly-fishing experiences, without a doubt.

443

Fish of the mountains

Alpine lakes, Sonamarg, Kashmir
May to September but beware of monsoon period
Trout

Sky-high lakes such as Gangabal, Vishansar and Krishansar hold trout, despite their altitude of more than 10,000 ft (3,000 m). Trout were brought here in colonial times and have flourished, even though these lakes are iced over for many months of the year. These are remote waters indeed and only accessed by trekking from the base in Sonamarg. The deep forests still hold bear and even snow leopard, so this is fly-fishing way off any beaten track. If you are agile with a burning desire for trout on the edge of the planet, this is for you.

444

Make new friends and catch prize fish in the Persian Gulf

Persian Gulf, Dubai, UAE
November to March
Barracuda, tuna, grouper

You'll find barracuda are plentiful year-round in the waters off Dubai, but for catching other popular prizes like tuna or grouper you'll be best off coming from November to about March. The waters here are spectacularly rich, and the fishing is an exciting way to connect with local guides and experience a different culture and customs, since fishing for many people here has been a way of life for generations.

445

A fly-fishing safari

Salalah, Dhofar, Oman
October to May
Permit and bream

The Omani coastline stretches for nearly 2,000 mi (3,218 km) and this is the chance to get out in a 4x4 and explore the rich shore-fishing available. Salalah is a terrific starting point with its stunning scenery and crystal waters close in. The peak target just has to be the permit, which are large and plentiful and can be caught especially on crab flies. The Oman bream are a great trophy fish too, however, along with queenfish, parrotfish, and milkfish that grow here in excess of 50 lb (22.5 kg). Oman prides itself on its hospitality and safety so this is a great opportunity to go it alone.

444 | **Angling and skyscrapers rarely marry as well as they do in Dubai**

446

Fishing crystal seas

Shuwaymiyah, Oman
October to April
Yellowfin tuna, giant trevally, amberjack

This incredibly remote area of Oman is worth a visit purely to see the camels and the stark desert landscapes, but the sea-fishing is also in a different league. The inshore fishing is excellent but get offshore to the Hallaniyat Islands and the giant trevally potential is massive with fish of more than 88 lb (40 kg) regularly caught. Yellowfin grow larger still and there is a strict conservation policy of "catch and release" to maintain these incredible stocks. There's also the chance to watch humpback whales and manta rays in this little-explored paradise.

447

A pioneering trip

Mountain rivers of Kyrgyzstan
Spring and fall
Trout species

Almost 90 percent of Kyrgyzstan is mountainous and many of the thousands of rivers are glacial. Known trout rivers include Red River, the Kekemeren, the Naryn, and the Chong-Kemin but there are many more, some relatively close to the capital Bishkek. Fly-fishing is in its infancy here so be prepared to experiment. You'll probably find types of brook trout, perhaps rainbows, and even the amudarya (a form of wild brown trout). There are also marinka, which look like the snow trout of the Himalayas. A wild, pioneering adventure awaits.

447 | **The wild rivers of mountainous Kyrgyzstan offer the chance to fish for trout**

448 | **Rudd look like pots of gold, splashed with red**

449 | **Ural river sturgeon are primeval creatures**

448

Submarines not fish

Ural Delta, Gureyev, Kazakhstan

Spring

Rudd

Twenty years ago, this delta was known for the enormous beluga sturgeon that entered the river to feast off spawning cyprinids in April and May. It was possible to hook fish in excess of 1,000 lb (450 kg). Today beluga are so persecuted for their caviar that they are on the Red List. However, in the swamps of this vast delta live some of the largest rudd on the planet. They can be caught in the 100 acre (40 hectare) lagoons on nymphs and dry flies and are barely credible for both their size and beauty.

449

Caspian giants

Ural River, Kazakhstan

April to September

Ship sturgeon

The ship sturgeon (also known as the fringebarbel sturgeon) lives in big places like the Black Sea, Aral Sea, and the Caspian Sea. In the Caspian, it lives alongside the great beluga sturgeon. They roam the Caspian Sea until they enter the Ural River and other rivers to spawn. The ship looks fairly similar to the beluga, the only visible difference being a white stripe along the bony scutes on its flanks. Also, it does not attain the same enormous weight as the beluga, but still reaches over 175 lb (79 kg). The best way to catch it, as with the beluga, is with a big piece of asp on a big, strong, single hook.

AUSTRALASIA

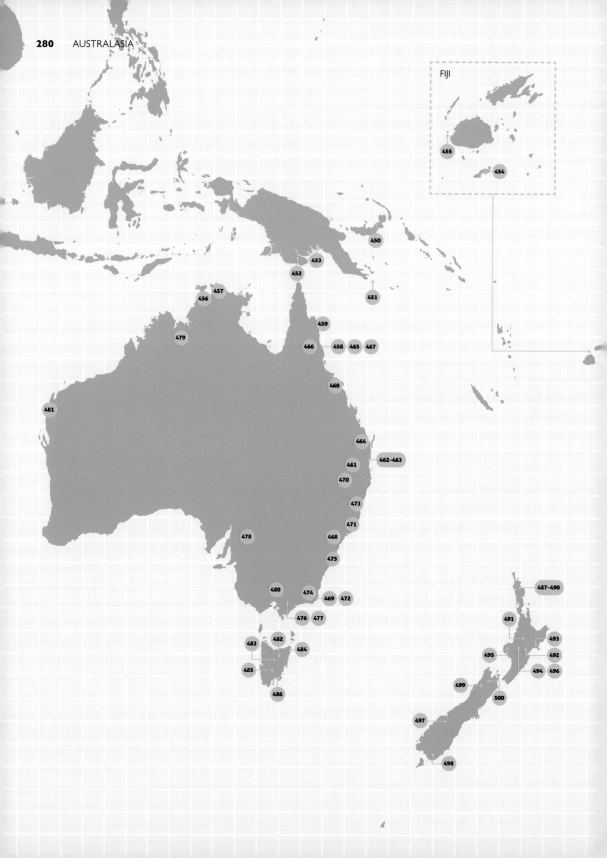

FIJI

455

454

450

453

452

451

456 457

479

459

466 458 465 467

460

481

464

461 462–463

470

473

471

478 468

475

480 474 469 472

476 477

483 482 484

485 487–490

486 491

493

495 492

494 496

499

500

497

498

AUSTRALASIA: ENTRY LIST

450 Baia, West New Britain, Papua New Guinea
451 Conflict Islands, Port Moresby, Papua New Guinea
452 Fly River, Western Province, Papua New Guinea
453 Kerema River, Gulf Province, Papua New Guinea
454 Kadavu Island, Fiji
455 Namotu Island, Fiji
456 Darwin, Northern Territory, Australia
457 South Alligator River, Kakadu National Park, Northern Territory, Australia
458 Trinty Inlet, Cairns, Queensland
459 Great Barrier Reef, Cairns, Queensland, Australia
460 Fitzroy River, Rockhampton, Queensland, Australia
461 Glenlyon Dam (Pike Creek Reservoir), Queensland, Australia
462 Southport, Gold Coast, Queensland, Australia
463 Gold Coast, Queensland, Australia
464 Lake Gregory, Bundaberg, Queensland, Australia
465 Mourilyan Harbour, Cassoway Coast, Queensland, Australia
466 Tinaroo Falls Dam, Queensland, Australia
467 Port Douglas, Queensland, Australia
468 Lake Lyell, Lithgow, Blue Mountains, New South Wales, Australia
469 Eden Harbour, New South Wales, Australia
470 Copeton Dam, Bingara, New South Wales, Australia
471 Port Stephens, New South Wales, Australia
472 Merimbula, Sapphire Coast, New South Wales, Australia
473 Macleay River, New South Wales, Australia
474 Snowy and Blue Mountains, New South Wales, Australia
475 Sydney, New South Wales, Australia

476 Blue Rock Lake, Melbourne, Victoria, Australia
477 Lake Eldon, Melbourne, Victoria, Australia
478 Murray River, Murray-Darling Basin, South Australia, Australia
479 Ord River, Kununurra, Western Australia, Australia
480 Queensland to Victoria, Australia
481 Ningaloo Reef, Exmouth Gulf, North West Cape, Western Australia, Australia
482 Meander River, North Deloraine, Tasmania, Australia
483 Nineteen Lagoons, Tasmania, Australia
484 St. Helens, Tasmania, Australia
485 Tyenna River, northwest of Hobart, Tasmania, Australia
486 Tasman Peninsula, Tasmania, Australia
487 Bay of Islands, North Island, New Zealand
488 Bay of Islands, North Island, New Zealand
489 Bay of Islands, North Island, New Zealand
490 Bay of Islands, North Island, New Zealand
491 Tongariro River, North Island, New Zealand
492 Mohaka River, near Napier, North Island, New Zealand
493 Lake Waikaremoana, Hawke's Bay, North Island, New Zealand
494 Rangitikei River, Wellington, New Zealand
495 Mount Taranaki, North Island, New Zealand
496 Taupo Lake, North Island, New Zealand
497 Ahuriri River, South Island, New Zealand
497 Mataura River, Invercargill, South Island, New Zealand
499 Buller River, near Nelson, South Island, New Zealand
500 Motueka River, South Island, New Zealand

450 | A majestic Papuan black bass

450

Get tooled up for action

Baia, West New Britain, Papua New Guinea
June to October
Papuan bass

This a tough location to reach, a good four hours by road from the nearest town of Kimbe, but there is a well-established lodge offering terrific hospitality. There are a variety of river systems here, all with world-class bass sport with fish that are absolute bruisers. Arm yourself with 50 lb (22.5 kg) braid mainlines, utterly reliable reels, 50 to 70 lb (22.5 to 32 kg) fluoro-carbon leaders, big tough lures, and you are in business. One final tip: check the hooks on your lures and replace if necessary, these can be the weak link that lets you down in the heat of combat.

451

Red-hot action

Conflict Islands, Port Moresby, Papua New Guinea
July to August, out of storm-season
November to May
Yellowfin tuna, billfish

Despite its name, this location is beyond every dream of what tropical-island life should be: white sandy beaches, crystal seas, coconut palms, turtles, and fish species beyond count. At Conflict, currents and topography combine to form a giant feeding station for all pelagic species. Here you'll find giant black marlin along with blue marlin, striped marlin, and swordfish. Yellowfin tuna are numerous and Spanish mackerel, giant trevally, dogtooth tuna, and others give red-hot action. There are even bonefish on the flats.

452

A mega fishing adventure

Fly River, Western Province, Papua New Guinea

July to November

Barramundi, black bass, giant trevally

Everything is oversized about this angling adventure. The river is huge, 652 mi (1,050 km) long, 31 mi (50 km) plus wide at the estuary, and even more than 0.6 mi (1 km) wide in its headwaters. It is estimated 128 fish species are found in the Fly and the colossal expanses of unspoiled flood plain are home to remote communities still with their own longstanding cultures and ways of life. The fish are startling. Bass here can reach over 40 lb (18 kg) and the barramundi can top 60 lb (27 kg) with ease. The colored water encourages lure-fishing and the story is that these fish fight like nowhere else.

The forests are home to the Raggiana bird-of-paradise

Giant trevally (GTs) infest the estuary

Apart from scattered settlements, you are alone

453

Tough trip for rich rewards
Kerema River, Gulf Province, Papua New Guinea
May to November
Papuan black bass

It could just be that the Kerema offers the best bass-fishing in the world, right at the point where the freshwater meets the sea. As the old maps said, here there be monsters, fish of 50 lb (22.5 kg), perhaps even more. Accessing the river is not easy, the road from Port Moresby has been challenging in the past, but the rewards are huge. If the bass are slow, there is first-class barramundi sport, along with bream species, jacks, and even giant trevallies. There is a rich culture here among the local people, too. Hook into one of these brutes of bass and your fishing world turns upside down.

454

A year-round fishing paradise
Kadavu Island, Fiji
**March and April for yellowfin tuna,
February to April for marlin, June to
August for wahoo, January to April for
giant trevally**
Yellowfin tuna, blue marlin, wahoo, giant trevally

Kadavu is one of a string of islands on an archipelago toward the south of Fiji. Few roads, no towns, lush rain forest, and abundant culture and wildlife all combine to make this a perfect destination. Here you'll find coral-fringed lagoons, miles of pristine reefs, and infinite fishing options in the crystal-clear seas. If there is a best time to fish, it might be January to May when the seas are generally calm. Yellowfin are plentiful around then, along with blue marlin, and enormous giant trevally that take popper-fishing to another level.

454 | Kadavu Island is a world of reefs, lagoons, and fish

455
The definition of paradise
Namotu Island, Fiji
All year
Marlin, yellowfin tuna, snapper, Spanish mackerel, Mali, giant trevally

There's always something to fish for inshore, offshore, or amid the reefs and lagoons of this angler's paradise. There are endless species in endless locations, such as Suva and Taveuni, all demanding different approaches. You can jig for yellowfin and mackerel; you can troll for marlin and Mali; fishing with poppers is hot for giant trevally especially in November and December; fly-fish for yellowfin even or go bottom-fishing for snappers and groupers. There's a whole year's fishing to be had in one of the most wondrous places on earth.

456
A fishing cornucopia
Darwin, Northern Territory, Australia
May to September
Barramundi

There's just so much to fish for around Darwin, but barra in the dry season is just about tops. Expect blue skies, light breezes, sensational sunsets, and, as the floodplains dry out, clearing water in the creeks, mangroves, and rivers. This clarity is ideal for the adventurous lure-angler who is faced with huge options. Fly-fishing comes into its own in the dry season, too. There is always a chance of a giant herring, a predatory sportfish that runs between 5 and 10 lb (2.3 and 4.5 kg). These can be stalked with a fly-rod and streamer-fly and then they fight with the aerial displays of a tarpon and the speed of a bonefish.

456 | A Darwin barramundi fights to the end

457

Top barra action

South Alligator River, Kakadu National Park,
Northern Territory, Australia
February to November
Barramundi

Kakadu is a pristine wetland of vast
proportions. It offers a huge waterscape, and
fishing is available in the rivers, creeks, and
billabongs of this deserted area. It is a
privilege to fish here and tight National Park
rules must be observed to maintain the
integrity of this wilderness. Also, do watch for
mudbanks and sandbars when afloat and if
shore-fishing keep 16 ft (5 m) back—take
saltwater crocs seriously. The absolute prime
time here is the run-off period between
February and April, but big catches of big
fish are landed season-long.

458 | **Trinity Inlet looks like a mirror at sunset**

458

Know your tides

Trinity Inlet, Cairns, Queensland
Warmer months
Barramundi

Trinity Inlet is a tropical, tidal estuary
covering 56 mi (90 km) and, in places, is
only a couple of minutes from the heart of
Cairns. Its urban proximity has made it a
favorite location but the barra fishing is
superb, too, providing you know your tides.
Basic rules are to fish deep water in slow
tides and shallow water in faster tides.
Generally, too, the best fishing is 1.5 hours
either side of either the high or low tide
mark. As with all barra fishing, local
knowledge is key, especially in finding the
structures that these fish love. Barramundi
are fish of the warmer months but Trinity
fishes well for giant trevally, bream, and
grunter in the colder months. Watch out for
crocs and the very dangerous box jellyfish.

459

Marlin marvels
Great Barrier Reef, Cairns, Queensland, Australia
September to mid-December
Black marlin

The Great Barrier Reef is all about superlatives. Apart from being a world-renowned location for marlin, it is the size of the Great Wall of China, reputedly visible from space, and home to 1,500 species of fish. The hub for visitors is Cairns, and the water between the town and Lizard Island is the dream location for marlin fanatics. Every season, fish of 1,000 lb (454 kg) are caught, often on the full moon or a week thereafter. Top techniques are lure and dead-bait trolling and fights can last for three full hours. A good job that some of the world's top skippers operate here.

460

Add it to your wish list
Fitzroy River, Rockhampton, Queensland, Australia
February 1 to November 1, but best in warmer months
Barramundi

Rockhampton is the self-styled "home of barramundi" and for good reason. It's said to be the only city in the world where you can fly in, check in, boat out, and be playing a specimen barramundi within a single hour. There is a huge variety of fishing here, in the main river, the tributaries, the lagoons, and in the delta itself. The city river is riddled with "barra boats" but there is plenty of bank fishing too—try the lagoons on the south side of the river or any of the many land-based sites such as Col Brown Park or Queen's Wharf. It might be urban but there are crocs about and the rare "bum-breathing turtle" . . . don't ask!

461 | **Murray cod caught at low light**

461

Nocturnal adventure

Glenlyon Dam (Pike Creek Reservoir),
Queensland, Australia
Summer and fall
Murray cod

At 4,324 acres (1,750 hectares), Glenlyon
is a vast reservoir, surrounded by woods and
rolling hills. The venue is known for smaller
species, notably golden perch, but the cod
here are huge and nationally famous. There
are endless creeks and inlets to explore and
you'll find plenty of sunken timber in these.
Low light is key and here is the place to try
an all-nighter. A boat is essential, as is an
electric motor, and extreme stealth. Choose
a calm night, preferably with little moon,
and work surface-lures to start. Takes are
confident, sometimes massive, and prepare
to be beaten up by these beasts of fish that
know how to fight to the end.

462

Striking gold

Southport, Gold Coast, Queensland, Australia
Summer months
Marlin

The Gold Coast has to be one of the
world's top saltwater destinations and
Southport is the epicenter of it all. It is
blessed with deep water close inshore
so big fish can be found within thirty
minutes of sailing time or less. During
spring and summer, smaller marlin
congregate in big numbers close inshore
and offer fabulous sport. If they are
feeding then wahoo, tuna, and mahi-mahi
are plentiful. Inshore fishing for cobia
and amberjack is easy to find especially
in the warmer months. Great fishing in
a spot that enjoys three-hundred days
of sunshine every year.

463

Annual marlin competition

Gold Coast, Queensland, Australia
December to September
Black marlin, blue marlin

The Gold Coast is a great tourist destination with its amazing beaches, but for marlin, it offers true magic and is one of the world-destinations for the species. The Gold Coast Game Fishing Club was formed over fifty years ago and organizes annual competitions here. Black marlin migrate down the east coast each year and congregate here on the Gold Coast from December, when several fish a day up to 200 lb (91 kg) plus are quite possible. There is top blue marlin sport as well with fish up to 600 lb (272 kg) plus taken by trolling, along with plentiful wahoo, dorado, and Spanish mackerel. Some of Australia's top skippers operate here.

463 | **Plentiful marlin add luster to the magic of the Gold Coast**

464
A hidden gem
Lake Gregory, Bundaberg, Queensland, Australia
Summer
Australian black bass

This is one of the lakes formed by the scores of water-storage dams in this area, sometimes called impoundments. Many offer cracking, accessible sport. Gregory is not massive, about 0.6 sq mi (1.6 sq km), and it's only around 10 ft (3 m) deep overall, but it is regularly and heavily stocked, so chances of a catch are high. It's off the beaten track, and a lure-fisher's paradise. Try noise-making lures, surface poppers, plastics, spinnerbaits, the lot. A kayak, or similar, gives you enviable command of reed- and weed-beds, lilies, and sunken timber, but also allows you to target the center of the lake where bass congregate.

465
Barra hotspot
Mourilyan Harbour, Cassoway Coast, Queensland, Australia
Summer
Barramundi

Mourilyan is situated around two hours south of Cairns. The tidal estuary here is a focus for barramundi once the water warms up. There is no river running into it so it does not flood or color during heavy rains making it a pretty reliable location. It's also a big system, best explored by boat. Mangrove channels, creeks, and sandbars are all fish-holding features. Fish with lures into mangrove roots, eddies, and around small islands. This is also jack-fishing heaven and in the cooler months giant trevally and queenfish come into their own.

464 | **Lake Gregory broods in the early morning mist**

465 | **Barramundi are the peak summer target**

466

Big barras aplenty

Tinaroo Falls Dam, Queensland, Australia

October to March

Barramundi

This massive dam was built in the 1950s and sits amid the lovely Atherton Tableland woodlands. The reservoir was stocked with barramundi and black bream in 1985 and both species have done phenomenally well. The freshwater has produced limitless big barras, including fish of 70 lb (32 kg) and more. The shoreline is 124 mi (200 km) long, so there is plenty of scope for bank-fishing, especially at sunrise and sunset. Look for all the usual fish-holding snags and structures, and it's a place where you can have success with fly as well as lure.

467

Mouthwatering variety

Port Douglas, Queensland, Australia

February to March for barramundi, June to August for red emperors, September to December for marlin

Barramundi, giant trevally, black marlin, red emperor

This has to be one of the world's saltwater-fishing hotspots. There are 225 listed sportfishing species to be pursued, seventy-five in the rivers and estuaries even. There is river-fishing, coastal-fishing, reef-fishing, game-fishing, and giant trevally-popper fishing. Anything you might want to catch, well, you'll find it here. This is also a tropical paradise where the Great Barrier Reef meets the Daintree rain forest and where there are 2,700 recorded hours of sunshine every year.

467 | **A black marlin soars in defiance**

The colors of the rainbow are entrancing

Spectacular sunset at Lake Lyell

Lyell browns reach trophy size

Lake Lyell is set in barren surroundings

468
Catch plentiful fish using a range of methods
Lake Lyell, Lithgow, Blue Mountains, New South Wales, Australia
Summer, but sport all year
Australian bass, rainbow trout, brown trout

This is a water-storage dam built forty years ago, so a slight word of warning is that occasionally levels can be low. Overall, though, Lyell is an accessible, attractive, and productive venue set in rolling countryside and just two hours from Sydney. A great plus is that you can troll, spin, bait, and fly-fish for plentiful fish, including trout up to 10 lb (4.5 kg). A kayak is a real boon here, allowing you to get to all the snaggy places, especially standing timber left over after the dam's flooding. Two tips: fish deep in the heat of the summer, but also try winter fly-fishing with wet flies, even when water is freezing the rod rings.

469
Saltwater bonanza
Eden Harbour, Sydney,
New South Wales, Australia
October to June
Yellowtail kingfish

Unlimited opportunities exist in Eden
Harbour, but especially kingfish which
at nearby Mowarry Point are found in big
sizes and big numbers. Their terrific fighting
qualities make them a huge favorite. But
in truth, there's everything to go at here.
Marlin are hot from December to May;
yellowfin tuna, albacore, and wahoo from
October to June; and snappers are inshore
favorites for much of the year. The deepwater navy wharf is another center for
most species but it can be busy during
holiday periods and can be closed
during maneuvers.

470
World-famous location
Copeton Dam, Bingara, New South
Wales, Australia
All year, but tough in winter
Murray cod

Copeton is a great jewel in the cod world.
It is said to cover three times the area of
Sydney Harbour, so while you won't be
alone, you won't feel pressured. The fish
here are awe inspiring. Murray cod of 3 ft
(1 m) plus are the target and three or four
fish a day of around that mark are recorded
by many anglers. It can be hard, and a start
before light is recommended. Remember the
three "S" words . . . surface baits, stickbaits,
and structure. You'll find miles of coves,
bays, rocky headlands, and submerged tree
stumps waiting to be attacked. Magnificent.

470 | Copeton is one of the many dams that make Australian fishing so dynamic

471 | **A Port Stephens shark contemplates its prey**

472 | **The rugged coastline along the Sapphire Coast**

471

Historic marlin grounds

Port Stephens, New South Wales, Australia
December to May for blue marlin, most of the year for striped marlin
Marlin, snapper

This truly is one of the red-hot game fishing destinations of the world. The Port Stephens Game Fishing Club has traditionally held the largest tournaments in the southern hemisphere for thousands of big fish enthusiasts. In part, the fabulous fishing is down to the Great Lakes Marine Park providing sanctuary zones, and a sensational fishing scene has grown up here. Big shark also feature in catches, and incredible dolphinfish and wahoo are a welcome bycatch when marlin-fishing. For casual fishing, the shore and estuary around the town also provide wonderful fishing on lighter gear.

472

Real scrappers of fish

Merimbula, Sapphire Coast, New South Wales, Australia
October to February
Yellowtail kingfish

The kingfish is an Australian favorite and its death-defying fight is as good a reason as any. These fish average 8 to 12 lb (3.6 to 5.4 kg) and swarm the Sapphire Coast as the waters warm. Merimbula is a pretty coastal town, a center of fishing activity, and has an artificial reef constructed not too far from the estuary. Reefs, along with rocks, headlands, and accumulations of prey fish, attract kings, but you have to hold on tight to keep them from snags and sanctuary. Top methods include vertical jigging, slow trolling, and throwing poppers at surface-feeding schools.

474 | Trout fishing the Thredbo River is all about cunning, caution, and calculation

473
Venue of two halves

Macleay River, New South Wales, Australia
Summer
Australian bass (up river); snapper, jewfish,
kingfish (at the estuary)

The Macleay runs for over 186 mi (300 km)
southeast from the Great Dividing Range,
and in its upper reaches is a magnificent
bass venue. High up, you'll find a clear
river with endless rapids and pools that
can be approached on foot or by kayak,
a craft that is especially useful in the deepest
areas where trolling is successful. Follow
the Macleay River Trail both for outstanding
access and natural beauty. When the river
reaches the sea, there is bountiful fishing
with incalculable species, perhaps the
favorite of which is the snapper. Popular
fishing spots are well publicized and rarely
fail to produce.

474
Serious sight fishing

Snowy and Blue Mountains, New South
Wales, Australia
October to June
Trout

This entry represents a wealth of top-class
fly-fishing for rainbow, brown, and even
brook trout in places. Moreover, we are
talking big fish, trophy fish in certain places,
that can be sighted, stalked, strategized, and
successfully landed. The Thredbo River is a
perfect example of an outstanding fishery
here: the river is self-sustaining and catch-
and-release is the way to keep it so. There
are also the nearby Blue Mountains, another
protected area riddled with secluded streams
and lakes. There are top-class guiding
services available that will enhance the
whole experience.

475

Fishing fun for all

Sydney, New South Wales, Australia

All year

Yellowtail, bream, flathead, trevally, snapper, Australian bass, carp, redfin, silver perch

If ever you find yourself in this fabulous city with a few hours (or days) to spare and a rod in hand, there are dozens of fishing spots available for the cost of a cheap license fee.

Most are saltwater but Manly Dam holds huge numbers of carp, silver perch, bass, and redfin. In the salt, where do you begin? Clarke's Point Reserve, Gunnamatta Bay, Gordon's Bay, Cook's River, Clifton Gardens, you can even fish Sydney Harbour with all the views that that entails; Blues Point Reserve offers some of the best. Even if you don't catch the fish of your dreams, it's an incredible experience.

475 | There aren't many more dramatic fishing locations than in Sydney itself

476

Redfin at the blue rock

Blue Rock Lake, Melbourne, Victoria, Australia

All year, but best in summer

Australian bass, trout, redfin

This is one of the best dam venues available
to the angler, particularly special because of
the mountainous backdrop. It's a great lake
for redfin, otherwise known as the European
perch. The species was introduced back in
the 1860s and it has flourished ever since.
While there are many redfin-aficionados,
perhaps the star attraction here is the bass,
and the favorite approach is to fish poppers
for fish fixated on terrestrial grasshoppers
and cicadas. Warm evenings in spring and
summer are especially "hot" and a kayak
is a massive benefit, as it is on many
storage lakes.

477

Murray magic

Lake Eldon, Melbourne, Victoria, Australia

All year, no closed season

Murray cod

Lake Eldon is situated in a lovely National
Park in the shadow of the Victorian Alps and
is another location for massive cod. The area
was the center of a gold rush back in the
1860s, but now it's the cod that are the
attraction, along with plentiful sightings of
kangaroos and wombats. It pays to move fast
and keep exploring new areas. Mix up your
lures and work them at different speeds.
Look for structure and for evidence of prey
fish, small redfins especially. A boat, as ever,
is useful but as the lake boasts 320 mi
(515 km) of shore, you are not going to
run out of bank access.

479 | **Barramundi are at their best along the Ord river**

478
Cod recovery
Murray River, Murray-Darling Basin,
South Australia, Australia
Summer and fall
Murray cod

First of all, let's say that there has been
something of an improvement in the
prospects for Murray cod in this vast river
system. In the recent past, the species was in
deep decline but the big fish still exist and
smaller cod between 1 and 10 lb (0.45 and
4.5 kg) are now coming back strongly. In
part, this is down to catch-and-release
attitudes adopted by anglers. The Basin
itself comprises 77,000 mi (123,919 km)
of waterways and covers more than 386,102
sq mi (1,000,000 sq km), so perhaps it is best
to concentrate on the Murray River—which
is itself 1,566 mi (2,520 km) long. However,
there are recognized fishing spots, like Lyrup
Flats, to get your adventure underway.

479
Big river barra
Ord River, Kununurra, Western Australia,
Australia
All year, though best in warmer months
Barramundi

The Ord is a serious river at 405 mi (651 km)
long, running through an all-but-deserted
landscape. Indeed, you're more likely to see
20 ft (6 m) crocs and kangaroos rather than
other humans, and plenty of barramundi,
of course. The lower Ord has well-known
hunting grounds, Skull Rock and Mambi
Island among them, and the best method
seems to be trolling lures so that you are
covering far more water than you can from
the bank. The river is frequently festooned
with snags, so top-water working lures can
be a safer bet than going deep.

Australia's signature fish: the mighty Murray cod is super impressive in every department

480
BUCKET LIST FISH: Murray cod
QUEENSLAND TO VICTORIA, AUSTRALIA

This enormous fish can grow to 200 lb (91 kg) and more. It is by far the largest of Australia's freshwater fish and it has a majestic beauty that wins lifetime converts to the species. Murray cod are not only massive but arm-wrenchingly strong and desperately difficult to fool, and these qualities more than qualify it for iconic status. Many of the large Australian storage reservoirs hold terrific "cod" but the Murray River is, perhaps, their spiritual home. It is heartening news that the species is, hopefully, making something of a comeback here after many years of decline.

481 | Swimming with whale sharks

482 | The Meander River has rapids, pools, and trout

481
Coral coast adventure
Ningaloo Reef, Exmouth Gulf, North West
Cape, Western Australia, Australia
March to October
Bonefish

North of Perth on Australia's west coast,
you'll find the pristine Ningaloo Reef which
lies a few hundred yards offshore, creating
boundless quiet lagoons and extensive sand
flats. The water here is crystal clear, the tidal
movement is small, and the sun generally
shines . . . in short, perfect bonefish stalking
conditions. The Exmouth Gulf lies to the
east of the reef and is mangrove-lined,
riddled with creeks and bonefish-filled flats.
Plentiful islands give you protection from
westerly winds and fishing conditions are
generally spot on. And, should the fishing
fun ever pall, you can always swim with
gigantic whale sharks.

482
Championship quality fish
Meander River, North Deloraine,
Tasmania, Australia
October to April
Trout

The World Fly-fishing Championship was
held on the Meander in 2019 and an English
angler commented it was like fishing in a zoo
there were so many fish. Both wild brown
and rainbow trout thrive in the cold clear
water that runs through both natural forest
and pleasant farmland. The upper beats
offer a tremendous diversity of riffles, runs,
and pools while lower down, the river
becomes a more placid meadow-stream.
Nymphing works well, but in the late
spring and summer there are great mayfly
and caddis hatches that tempt the fish
to the surface.

483

Trout stalking supreme
Nineteen Lagoons, Tasmania, Australia
Spring to fall
Trout

Lying in the region of the western lakes, the Nineteen Lagoons are made up of a bewildering array of big lakes, smaller pools, creeks, streams—even puddles of water seem to hold big trout. This is all about getting rugged. Pull on your boots and get walking, investigating, and, above all, watching. Look for that monster trout you can stalk, strategize, and perhaps even catch. The waters are cold in the spring when the fish are hungry but the summer sees big fly hatches. You are in the Tasmanian Wilderness, which is a World Heritage Area, so look out for wombats, wallabies, and even the odd platypus.

484

Action on the Bay of Fires
St. Helens, Tasmania, Australia
December to June for big game,
November to June for shore-fishing
Marlin, tuna

This charming little town situated on the northeast side of the island is often described as the headquarters of Tasmanian sea-fishing. It is just south of the Bay of Fires and both the land and the seas around are sheltered and legally protected. This has resulted in exceptionally clear waters, rich in water grasses, reefs, lagoons, and fish. You can fish the shore from the pier, in the bay, or along the estuary for a variety of species including sea bream and garfish. Charter boats can deliver rich sport with tuna, marlin, mako shark, swordfish, and kingfish.

484 | The coast is rich in bays, reefs, lagoons, and fish

485
Tasmania's top trouting
Tyenna River, northwest of Hobart, Tasmania, Australia
August to April
Brown trout, rainbow trout

The Tyenna is a jewel, perhaps the most popular trout venue on the island. It is run as a wild brown trout fishery and is colossally prolific, one survey suggesting that there are 150 fish for every 328 ft (100 m) of river. If that were not enough, there are also rainbow trout reaching a large size. A stretch of water runs through Mountfield National Park and here only fly-fishing is allowed. Wading is easy and productive as the river is generally shallow with many rapids and streamy runs. Upstream-nymphing seems to be a favorite tactic, and there are big caddis hatches on warm evenings which get the fish up.

487
Angler's El Dorado
Bay of Islands, North Island, New Zealand
February and March
Marlin

Big-game fishing in the Bay of Islands was put onto the world map largely by author Zane Grey, who spent his fortune fishing the world. He named the Bay "the Angler's El Dorado," and for good reason. His fisherman's log of 1927 makes for awesome reading, including the account of his record 704 lb (319 kg) marlin. It's a short window for these giant fish, but charters are available, invariably of high quality. There are 144 islands in the bay so there is a vast variety of water to investigate. Sightings of albatross, penguin, dolphin, and orca only increase the drama of this location.

486
Bluefin drama
Tasman Peninsula, Tasmania, Australia
April to late June
Southern bluefin tuna

What drama you can have with bluefins around this striking coastline. Port Arthur, Pirates Bay, and Fortescue Bay are all launching points if you have your own boat and don't need the services of the excellent local skippers. Top marks include Hippolyte Rocks, Tasman Island, and Lanterns where trolling on rough days generally sees the best results. At times, school fish in the 30 to 50 lb (13 to 22.5 kg) range swarm here, providing amazing sport if you hit it right. Much bigger fish are also fished, sometimes just a little later in the season.

486 | The drama of the Tasmanian coast reaches its climax around the Totem Pole headland

They may not be great whites, but all Bay of Island shark scrap until they're in the boat

488
BUCKET LIST FISH: Shark
BAY OF ISLANDS, NEW ZEALAND

There are around 400 species of shark worldwide, ranging from 2 ft (60 cm) long to thirty times that. The smaller end of the shark family tree certainly merits angling attention. Spurdog is a shore angler's favorite, and tope-fishing is riveting stuff on lighter gear. Some intrepid types are even catching 50 lb-ers (22.5 kg) from kayaks out in the North Sea on fly-gear. At the top end, size-wise, it is important to note that many shark species are now off limits, and restrictions are tight to conserve epic fish such as the great white. However, blue, mako, porbeagle, and bull shark are all thrilling enough, to name just four out of many.

The albatross is the greatest angler of all

489
The speed merchants
Bay of Islands, New Zealand
All year, best late summer through fall
Kingfish

Mention Bay of Islands—"discovered" and named by Captain Cook in 1769—and anglers think big-game fishing, but the fighting kingfish here are in a league of their own. Yellowtail "kingis" are only found in the southern hemisphere and the largest variety and numbers swim around the shores of New Zealand. Kingfish meccas such as Cape Brett, Hanson's Reef, and Kingfisher Reef are legendary and most fish are taken on trolled live bait. However, extra long jigs that mimic injured fish are now proving almost equally effective. Keep your eyes open for albatross, shearwaters, and little blue penguins in this magical place.

A sleek kingfish glides through the waters

Urapukapuka is one of the many unforgettable islands

490

Great sport under the eye of an albatross

Bay of Islands, North Island, New Zealand
Spring to early summer for snapper, late summer to fall for kingfish
Snapper, kingfish

Inshore fishing around the Bay of Islands is almost a national obsession. There are so many fishing points, so many opportunities, and so many fish. Because of the number of islands and headlands, there are always places to fish that are out of the wind. Snapper average perhaps 4 lb (1.8 kg) and are universally prolific. They taste fantastic with a chilled white wine. Kingfish are much the larger species and fight with legendary power. They can be caught on lure but for fish of more than 40 lb (18 kg) jack-mackerel type baits are generally used. Troll or drift these or use straight ledger gear.

491

River of monster rainbows

Tongariro River, North Island, New Zealand
All year
Rainbow trout, brown trout

This is Lake Taupo's largest tributary and it flows through volcanic scenery of raw beauty. The river is wide, swift, and intimidating, powering its way over rocks, sand, and gravel. The type of fishing changes with the seasons, but winter is hugely popular as thousands of trout leave the lake to spawn in the river. These are big fish averaging 4.4 lb (2 kg) and especially large ones can be found in the pools. In summer, the banks are quieter and the plentiful fish fall to all manner of nymph techniques; French-leader work is especially productive.

490 | A kingfish plunges for freedom

491 | The Tongariro is one of the great trout rivers

492
A New Zealand gem
Mohaka River, near Napier, North Island,
New Zealand
October to April
Rainbow trout, brown trout

This lovely river is one of the North Island's
gems. In the lower reaches, fishing is easier
and the trout gather to gorge on whitebait
at certain times of the year. The upper
reaches are something else, however. Here,
you can seek out barely fished spots if you
are prepared to hike . . . or splash out on a
helicopter. You can spin in places, but
fly-fishing is preferred and the dry fly-fishing
in summer can be exceptional. Huge browns
of 10 lb (4.5 kg) or so—trophy fish indeed—
exist in the upper reaches and are prolific
after heavy beech-seeding years when the
mouse population explodes.

493
Sea of rippling water
Lake Waikaremoana, Hawke's Bay,
North Island, New Zealand
October to June
Trout

Lake Waikaremoana is situated at 1,903 ft
(580 m) of altitude in the high hills of the
Te Urewera National Park. The water is
up to 656 ft (200 m) deep and crystal-clear,
a feature that might date back 2,000 years
when the lake was created by a huge
landslide. Waikaremoana is known as a
dry-fly venue and the trophy browns are
famously stalked around the margins of the
shoreline. Big rainbows are generally taken
farther out when afloat—but these are
generalizations only. The lake is entered
by limitless streams and some of these can
fruitfully be fished.

492 | **The upper reaches of the Mohaka River**

493 | **Lake Waikaremoana is home to trophy trout**

494

Ten pounders in pristine headwaters

Rangitikei River, Wellington, New Zealand

November to April

Rainbow trout, brown trout

This 150 mi (241 km) long river has its headwaters in the remote Kaimanawa Forest Park, which is an enchanting landscape of bush-clad hills. The fishing here is all about the pristine headwaters, for which you will need to apply for a free-of-charge back-country fishing license. The river here is a mix of deep pools, glittering rapids, and glides, while the water runs a tantalizing shade of bottle green. It is possible to fish 10 lb (4.5 kg) trophy trout here, but beware of fast-changing weather conditions and remember a two-hour hike gets you to the furthest and best beats.

495

A plethora of rivers

Mount Taranaki, North Island, New Zealand

October to April

Rainbow trout, brown trout

The fishing here is centered around the Egmont National Park, a quiet, scenic paradise rich in native trees and lush, green meadows. There are several trout-filled lakes in the region but the forty or more rivers and streams give Taranaki its uniqueness. These are crystal streams, off the radar, and so experience little angling pressure. One of the prime rivers is the Waingongoro, home to double-figure rainbows and a self-sustaining population of brown trout. The angler who travels light and is prepared to put in the hiking, is the successful angler here.

495 | **Fishing in the reflection of Mount Taranaki**

496
The historic home of New Zealand trouting
Taupo Lake, North Island, New Zealand
All year
Rainbow trout, brown trout

This 238 sq mile (616 sq km) lake has to be the most famous trout still water in the world. The scenery is breathtaking, and the 607 ft (185 m) deep water a crystal blue. The trout probably average 3 lb (1.4 kg) but many 11 lb (5 kg) fish are taken every year. Each season of the year calls for different approaches and it is hard to settle on a "best" time, though in the spring, the smelt spawn in the shallows and the very big fish come in close to gorge on their prey. Fly-fishing is popular but jigging, trolling, and harling are all practiced from well-skippered boats.

497 | The green-blue waters of the Ahuriri River flow from the mountains and breed trout that fish like banshees

497
Trophy trout in mountain river
Ahuriri River, South Island, New Zealand
December to April
Rainbow trout, brown trout

The upper reaches of the Ahuriri are of international conservational importance. Consequently, the fly-only rule is in place for the Ahuriri River, which runs through the park. The river runs through a vast plain, bordered on both sides by towering mountains. Winds can be challenging but who cares when faced with such a glorious trout stream? It runs with that delectable shade of green-blue all trout fishers recognize, and the browns especially are magnificent. It's not just that they are big—trophy fish are numerous—but also that they are magnificently shaped and spotted, and fight like banshees. As ever, breathable waders allow you to walk the distances necessary.

498
Bountiful mayfly and evening rises
Mataura River, Invercargill, South Island, New Zealand
October to April
Brown trout

All these South Island rivers are gems but they are all subtly different. The Mataura, for instance, is famous for its mayfly hatches and for sport on the dry fly. The river is reputed to hold the highest density of trout of any river in New Zealand, and the mid and lower sections around the town of Gore are hugely popular. However, purists would advise exploring the upper reaches: rich in willow-lined pools and deep marginal undercuts. The water here has been described not just as "gin," but as "double distilled gin" and that is why fishing into evening and dusk often brings the only sport of the day.

499 | A brown trout about to be released back into the river near Owen River Lodge near Nelson

499
Unbelievable brown trout
Buller River, near Nelson, South Island,
New Zealand
October to April
Brown trout

What a true delight this river is, about
100 mi (160 km) long, running out of
Rotoiti Lake. It is one of the country's havens
for brown trout, with averages close to 3 lb
(1.4 kg) and present in big numbers. The
scenery throughout is a trout lover's dream
and there is little not to love. It's best to
avoid the lower section, which is deeper,
slower, and more suited to spinner. The
middle beats of the river are open-banked,
easy-paced, and straightforward to fish but
it is the upper Buller that is the best.
Narrow, fast, clear, and a real fly fisher's
challenge. Plenty of fish though and what
a fight in that current.

500
Sight-fishing supreme
Motueka River, South Island, New Zealand
October to December
Brown trout

This could be the best river for brown trout
in all of New Zealand, which many would say
is quite some claim! This glorious river is
barely an hour from Nelson. While its
accessibility can be an advantage, it also
means that it's prone to crowds in summer.
The early part of the season is considered
prime, after a winter with no angling
pressure and steady, rich feeding. Toward
the mouth of the river, there are frequent
catches of sea-run browns but for the very
biggest fish of all, get yourself way upstream.
Here, there is spectacular sight-fishing for
fish sometimes in excess of 5 lb (2.3 kg).

INDEX

INDEX

INDEX

PICTURE CREDITS

The publisher would like to thank the following for the permission to reproduce copyright material.

(T) Top; (B) Bottom; (L) Left; (R) Right; (C) Center; (TL) Top left; (TR) Top right; (BL) Bottom left; (BR) Bottom right.

Alamy: 34/35, 61 Cavan Images; 73 (B) sablin; 90 Joana Kruse; 101 Luciano Candisani/ Minden Pictures; 126 (R) Yvette Cardozo; 144 imageBROKER; 151 Stewart Collingswood; 158 Prisma by Dukas Presseagentur GmbH; 164 sablin; 183 Jeff Tucker/ Stockimo; 184 (TL) Jim Laws; 190 (R) H2O-images; 196 Biosphoto; 203 Henry Gilbey; 204 (TR) John Warburton-Lee Photography; 204 (B) Martin Mwaura; 205 Westend 61 GmbH; 219 Les Gibbon; 223 Minden Pictures; 238 (TL) Newscom; 238 (TR) Xinhua; 264 sablin; 266/267 Hemis; 269 Ville Palonen; 283 (BR) Neil Bowman; 289 redbrickstock.com/Andrew Shield.

Bahamas Ministry of Tourism: 62/63; 83; 84/85; 86.

John Bailey: 148 (L); 271.

Bale Mountains Eco Trekking Tours, https://www.balemountainsecotrekking.com: 201.

Blue Safari Seychelles, www.bluesafari.com: 4/5; 9; 10; 87 Trevor Sithole; 210 (L); 210 (R) Rudolph Lubbe; 211, 212 Brian Chakanyuka.

Catamaran Cruises Mauritius, www.catamaran-cruises.com: 209 (R).

Rhys Creed of Social Fishing, https://socialfishing.com.au/: 288; 299.

Flickr: 16 Andrew Feicht; 22 Amarneejill; 23 USFWS/ Andrew Gilham; 31 (R) Tim Donovan; 37 Florida Fish and Wildlife; 39 Image Tek; 43 Becky Dee; 50 (R) USFWS/Justin Dummit; 51 (R) Jeff Bailey; 54 (L) 54 USDS; (R) USFWS/Paula Gouse; 55 USDA Photo by Preston Keres; 78 (L) Michael Stockton; 182 Public Domain; 214 (R) South African Tourism; 238 (B) Christopher John; 245 (T) Jonathan Vail; 276 Prashant Ram; 298 Jon Connell; 306 (L) Andym5855.

Getty Images: 2/3 Stewart Sutton; 12/13 Rubberball Productions; 24 Jonathan Tucker/Stocktrek Images; 32 Miami Herald; 36 Mauricio Handler; 46 (B) Tony Aruzza; 60 (R) Ronald C Modra; 70 Rodrigo Friscione; 81 Mauricio Handler; 88/89 The Washington Post; 108/109 Andrew Geiger; 118 (BR) Tony Arruza; 224 (C) Sam Diephuis; 230/231 View Pictures; 265 Richinpit; 278/279 Pekic; 291 THEPALMER; 294 (L) Ryan Sault/EyeEm.

Istockphoto: 17 cuphoto; 56 KeithSzafranski; 60 (L) studio-laska; 67 (R) stammphoto; 74 (B) pilesasmiles; 98 (TL) Roi Shomer; 160 Ian Sheriffs; 162 stephankerkhofs; 174/175 daverhead; 209 (L) vale_t; 213 Louis-Michel Desert; 222 Oleona; 239 gyro; 284 Christian Herzog.

Johnny Jensen: 19 (L); 19 (R); 126 (L); 129 (R); 168 (R); 173 (L); 224 (B); 250 (BL); 250 (BR); 258 (TR); 273 (L); 290 (R).

Mauritia Kirchner, Flyfishing Publications, www.falklandislandsfly.fishing: 111.

Lake Lyell Recreation Park: 292 (TL); 292 (TR).

Kevin Morlock: 57.

Mark Murray, www.africanwaters.net (Angler: Jill Calitz): 206 (R).

Nxamaseri Island Lodge: 218 (TL); 218 (TR); 218 (B).

Owen River Lodge, www.OwenRiverLodge.co.nz: 311.

Shutterstock: 6 Semachkovsky; 14 (Main pic) Ad_hominem; 14 (BL) Elena_Titova; 18 Michal Onderco; 20 (TL) Richard Paksi; 20 (TR) CSNafzger; 20 (B) EB Adventure Photography; 21 Nate Grangroth; 25 (L) Iryna Harry; 25 (R) Fuss Sergey; 27 Yena Lou; 29 Kellis; 30 (L) Norman Bateman; 30 (R) CLP Media; 31 (L) Ruth Peterkin; 33 The Floridian; 38 Tailored Media; 40 Nat Chittamai; 41 (L) DanVanPelt; 41 (TR) LivyGrace; 41 (BR) DeepGreen; 44 Matt Jeppson; 45 Alessandro De Maddalena; 46 (T) Impassioned Images; 47 (L) Jeff Stamer; 47 (R) Kwanza Henderson; 48 Gorb Andrii; 51 (L) liveyourlife; 52 SnapTPhotography; 58 Connor Howe; 64 (Main pic) Inkiart; 64 (inset) Save nature and wildlife; 64 (BL) skvoor; 66 Diego Grandi; 67 (L) FIMP; 68 Yuriy Y.Ivanov; 69 Jason Richeux; 71 (BL) Ondrej Prosicky; 70 (BC) Uwe Bergwitz; 70 (BR) Diego Grandi; 71 (T) Cesar Gonzalez Palomo; 72 Rio De Luz; 73 (T) Milosz Maslanka; 74 (T) Fabien Monteil; 75 Diego Grandi; 76 (L) lomingen; 76 (R) reisegraf.ch; 77 (TL) Photofenik; 77 (TR) rvb3ns; 78(R) John McMahon; 79 (L) U. Eisenlohr; 79 (R) Digital Blue; 80 Stefan Neumann; 82 (L) Travis Boughton; 82 (R) Kwanza Henderson; 91 (L) rustamxakim; 91 (R) MevZup; 92 Phil O'nector; 94 Kwanza Henderson; 95 Jason Richeux; 96 ByDroneVideos; 97 Bignai; 98 (TR) Vinicius Bacarin; 98 (B) Vinicius Bacarin; 99 Nature's Charm; 100 Luciana Tancredo; 102 Patricia Matias Geo; 103 Patricia Matias Geo; 104 Valentin Ayupov; 105 (L) Ana Gram; 105 (R) Viniciussouza06; 107 COULANGES; 110 Tarcisio Schnaider; 112 Erik Klietsch; 117 (BL) Curioso Photography; 117

Special thanks to the following individuals, organisations and tour companies.

African Waters
www.africanwaters.net

Amazon Antonio Jungle Tours and Antonio Gomes
www.antonio-jungletours.com

Bale Mountains Eco Trekking Tours
www.balemountainsecotrekking.com

Blue Safari Seychelles
www.bluesafari.com

alphonse-island.com
www.alphonsefishingco.com

Catamaran Cruises Mauritius
www.catamaran-cruises.com

Flyfishing Publications and Mauritia Kirchner
www.falklandislandsfly.fishing

Peru Anglers and Gabriel Gygax
www.peruanglers.com

Rock Expeditions
www.rockexpeditions.com

AUTHOR BIOGRAPHIES

John Bailey

John Bailey is an experienced fishing guide, author, photographer, and TV consultant. He has fished in more than sixty countries, catching iconic species including mahseer in India, taimen in Mongolia, and Arctic char beneath the glaciers of Greenland. He has written more than fifty books as well as numerous angling articles for newspapers and magazines. John's expertise as a guide keeps him busy on his local waters in the UK, and he has worked as the fishing consultant on a range of movies and TV shows, most recently the BBC's *Mortimer and Whitehouse: Gone Fishing.* John lives near the beautiful River Wye in England.

Ray Bartlett

Ray Bartlett is a travel writer and novelist who specializes in the Americas, Asia, and other parts of the globe. His work has appeared in numerous publications, including *Lonely Planet* and other guidebooks, as well as newspapers, magazines, public radio, and online. He is the author of two novels, *Sunsets of Tulum* and *Celadon.* When not on the road somewhere, he divides his time between the US, Mexico, and Japan, often with a fishing rod in hand.

Rob Beattie

Rob Beattie first went fishing when he was ten years old and last went fishing yesterday. He's the author of more than twenty books, including *The 101 Golden Rules of Fishing, The Bluffer's Guide to Fishing,* and *Fishing: A Very Peculiar History.* A long-time contributor to *Waterlog* magazine in the UK, Rob plays and sings with the Alter Eagles tribute band and lives in Sussex, near his beloved River Adur.

Kiki Deere

Kiki Deere's fishing exploits range from piranha fishing in the Amazon to trout fishing on Scotland's western isles. Her work has been published in major travel publications including *The Telegraph, Condé Nast Traveller,* and *Culture Trip.* You'll find her exploring the great outdoors or tucking into culinary specialties to discover local flavors. Instagram and Twitter: @kikideere

Johnny Jensen

Johnny Jensen is a sportfishing writer and photographer who has visited more than thirty countries with his fishing rod and camera. He has contributed to more than twenty magazines and fifty books, including *Dreamfishing,* his photographic account of fishing around the world, published in Denmark in 2010. www.JJPhoto.dk

The authors and publishers are very grateful to Ian Whitelaw for his valuable input at the start of this project.